"Reading *There Is a Way* is like
wise, trusted friend. Birthed from
counselor, C. Dennis Kaufman offers a refreshing take on spiritual formation—a bridge between ordinary life and the vibrant experience with God we long for. Through his case studies, we see hope for ourselves to find the way to thriving life, and his questions invite us to actively step forward on that path."

—**Andrew "Fitz" Fitzgibbon**, lead minister, Okolona Christian Church

"I have met numerous people that are struggling with becoming who they feel God intends them to be. They are stuck in difficult circumstances with no real plan to move towards the growth they desire. In *There Is a Way*, C. Dennis Kaufman provides practical strategies that have grown from his own spiritual dedication and clinical expertise. Following this wisdom will move you closer to the person you are working to become!"

—**Aaron W. Banister**, licensed psychologist

"I have known C. Dennis Kaufman as a friend and colleague for over thirty years. A seasoned pastor and therapist, Kaufman takes the word of God seriously while applying it graciously to our lives. He knows about brokenness, about hurt, about desperately wanting and needing to be someone that we are not. Few books offer a gentle but firm hand to travel this poorly lit path. Deep and yet accessible, this book is a true gem. I highly recommend it!"

—**James P. Kassel**, licensed psychologist

There Is a Way

There Is a Way

Nine Vital Skills for an
Excellent Christian Journey

C. Dennis Kaufman

FOREWORD BY
Bob Russell

RESOURCE *Publications* · Eugene, Oregon

THERE IS A WAY
Nine Vital Skills for an Excellent Christian Journey

Resource Publications
An Imprint of Wipf and Stock Publishers
199 W. 8th Ave., Suite 3
Eugene, OR 97401

www.wipfandstock.com

PAPERBACK ISBN: 978-1-6667-7215-9
HARDCOVER ISBN: 978-1-6667-7216-6
EBOOK ISBN: 978-1-6667-7217-3

07/03/23

Contents

Foreword

W hen we put our trust in Christ, God grants us the gift of salvation. That is what God did for us. That is instantaneous. But from that moment on we are to grow to become like Christ—we're not to remain spiritual infants. Christ wants to transform us into his image. He wants to mature the way we think, feel, and behave every day. That's what we do for him, and it takes a lifetime!

Simon Peter, who was himself dramatically transformed by Christ over a period of time, wrote, "Make every effort to add to your faith goodness; and to goodness, knowledge; and to knowledge, self-control; and to self-control, perseverance; and to perseverance, godliness; and to godliness, mutual affection; and to mutual affection, love" (2 Pet 1:5–7).

Dennis Kaufman's insightful book *There Is a Way* is designed to help readers mature in their faith in God and deepen in their understanding of others. You'll find Dennis's knowledge of God's word and his experience with people who have gone through struggles beneficial in enhancing your personal walk with Christ. Dennis integrates biblical truth with psychological principles and practical application. He tactfully illustrates the truth of each chapter with an anonymous and fascinating case study straight out of his personal experience as a counselor.

FOREWORD

The title of this book comes from Jesus's words: "For the gate is narrow and the way is hard that leads to life, and those who find it are few" (Matt 7:14 ESV). Before they were labeled "Christians" the first believers were called "People of the Way." That "way" is often difficult and sometimes dangerous. But his way leads to an eternal and abundant life. When we travel the rugged road marked out for us, we develop spiritual muscles and grow to be like Jesus, who from childhood "grew in wisdom and stature, and in favor with God and man" (Luke 2:52).

I came to know Dennis Kaufman well when we served on staff together at Southeast Christian Church in Louisville, Kentucky. Dennis is one of those people who the more you learn about them, the more you respect them. Initially he was very unassuming and willing to stay out of the limelight even though he had previously been the lead pastor of a church. He was supportive and uncritical of my leadership even though he had been an effective leader himself. Dennis was humble and willing to fill any position that was needed at the time even though that occasionally meant extra preparation in an area that was new to him. He did everything well and soon everyone on staff held Dennis Kaufman and his family in high esteem.

Eventually we learned Dennis's finest gifts were in counseling and one-on-one encounters. People instinctively had confidence in him and easily opened up to him because of his gentle nature. His biblical counsel is solid; he is an excellent listener and wise confidant. People who were struggling trusted him to keep confidences and that trust was justified. Dennis has a wealth of knowledge about the Bible but his years as a counselor have instilled in him a keen understanding of people. Like Jesus, Dennis Kaufman is "full of grace and truth" (John 1:14).

I am confident Dennis's book will help readers "add to their faith" and bring about a "mutual affection" for others. Simon Peter promises the result of growing in Christian character is this: "For if you possess these qualities in increasing measure, they will keep you from being ineffective and unproductive in your knowledge of our Lord Jesus Christ" (2 Pet 1:8).

A familiar plaque bearing the words of Hans Urs von Balthasar reminds us, "What you are is God's gift to you, what you become is your gift to God." Reading *There Is a Way* will assist you in giving back to the One who has given so much to you because "there is a way that leads to life."

Bob Russell

February 2023

Acknowledgments

To publish a book on the backside of a long career automatically means there have been many, many people along the way that played a part in my life experiences that helped construct this study. There are three groups of people that stand out to me that I would like to give credit for their encouragement, steady support, and inspiration.

First, there is my family. Every therapist knows the power of a stable environment during those developmental years. John and Betty Kaufman loved their three boys, of which I was the middle. No middle child jokes, please. Not a day has gone by where my parents' support has not been felt. Having a family of your own also creates endless possibilities for growth and insight. Denise is my wife of forty-seven years. She is both the love of my life and an awesome proofreader, a sweet combination when taking on a project like this. My two daughters, Jennifer Leach and Sarah Longest, are delightful young women of whom I am so proud. It has been an amazing adventure to watch them grow up, establish their own faith, and pour into their families. I only wish they more fully appreciated my "dad jokes."

Second, there are my teachers and colleagues. I remember Cy Stocke, Dr. James Kurfees, Dr. Wayne Oates, and Dr. James

Hyde. These four sages saw something in me as a young pastor and provided astute guidance and supervision as I found my way through the long process of becoming a licensed pastoral counselor and launched into the world of Christian therapy. My faithful colleagues like Don Delafield, Linda Allen, Kurt Sauder, and Dr. James Kassel have prayed and agonized and laughed with me as we have been in the trenches together looking for ways to help people grow one at a time for all these years. I am also very grateful for Dr. Aaron Banister and Ian Wooldridge. These two young men have faithfully read my chapters as they were written, and provided feedback from a younger generation, which I deeply respect. Both are excellent writers themselves, and I encourage you to be on the lookout for works they may publish in the future. Also, Ruth Schenk has come alongside me in the writing process to encourage me, introduce me to the world of publishing, and provide great editorial advice.

Last but certainly not least, there are all those people who have trusted me as their counselor, pastor, teacher, or mentor. There is nothing that facilitates spiritual formation and development more than getting to share what you are learning with others. To be trusted by people and have them send others your way for counsel is the ultimate compliment and encouragement. When people share their stories, the space where you are sitting begins to feel like sacred ground. For those of us who are endlessly curious about human beings, this work never gets old.

The nine case studies you will read in this book are but a small sampling of my deep appreciation for all who have extended the privilege to enter their world and experience the uniqueness of their journeys. God obviously knew the wisdom of encouraging us to build community and to learn how to take care of each other. This book is dedicated to spur each other on toward the abundant life that is available because of the good news that God delivered through Jesus.

Introduction

As I sit here today reflecting on forty-plus years of pastoral care and counseling, I feel incredibly blessed to have watched God work in the lives of so many people. It is an amazing thing to observe a person's life unfold before you in such a close-up and personal way. It is also a little overwhelming to think about trying to describe the subtle and intangible ways that this life journey with God takes place. But that is one of the goals of this study. Since communicating these observations is no easy task, I hope to use all the tools at my disposal to help you get a sense of how we get from where we are to where we want to be on this incredible trek called life. So, each chapter will contain biblical concepts, psychological theory, a case study, and analogies; all designed to help us see as clearly as we can that unseen world of the faith journey.

After two thousand years, the profound words of Jesus still reverberate through our world: "I am the way and the truth and the life" (John 14:6). Millions of us believe that our Christian faith is the best way to an abundant life, and yet there is a fair amount of evidence that many churches and individual believers can live their lives in the same old ruts and patterns that defined them years ago. We bump into those pesky statistics that clearly seem to indicate that things like divorce rates, pornography use, and "less-than-kind" driving habits are not all that different between Christians and non-Christians. We must admit that the church has not always been a shining star in its testimony to a broken world.

In this day and time, followers of Jesus face a formidable challenge in trying to harmonize our deeply held belief that the gospel is incredibly powerful with the everyday experience that many who profess it seem to be relatively unchanged by it. What are your hunches as to why something as powerful as the gospel can have so little impact on the way people live their lives?

We could conclude that God's word is inaccurate in the way it portrays the impact of the gospel, but we would be wrong. We could also just blame the discrepancy on the pitiful efforts of Christ's followers. But that would just create more shame and guilt which tends to be demoralizing and unproductive. The Bible is clear that the real challenge we face is the integration of spiritual truths into our earthly existence. The Hebrew writer uses the language of mixing our experience with faith (Heb 4:2 KJV). This is no small endeavor. Paul makes it clear in Rom 6–8 that the invitation we extend to God to take up residence within us creates nothing short of a civil war between our sinful nature and the Spirit of God.

Because this integration process is so uncomfortable, we often find a way to short-circuit it and we are left with our old, more comfortable ways of doing life that do not reflect the changes God intends. We have underestimated the difficulty of moving from "my will be done" to "thy will be done." Perhaps this is the reason Jesus himself indicated that few would find this narrow road that leads to life (Matt 7:13–14).

As we use words like uncomfortable, difficult, and narrow, it is not unusual to begin to feel like the Christian life is all about trying and striving, but this is where our faith is different than all others. As we will see throughout this book, the challenge Jesus gives us can only be met by a growing understanding of grace and God's patience with us as we learn to live by faith. Through the centuries, religious people have often made the mistake of setting legalistic standards for people that cannot be met. With this added pressure, we tend to either chronically feel bad about our shortcomings (shame) or alter reality and deceive ourselves into thinking we are further along than we really are (pride). This was the pitfall of the religious leaders in Jesus's day. They thought they were holier than others, but in all reality, they were a spiritual mess. When Jesus pointed this out, he incurred their wrath.

Have you ever felt like you had to be less than honest about yourself in a church setting to fit in or be accepted? How would that affect our sense of emotional safety and the ability to truly be accountable regarding our struggles? The gospel truly is the most powerful, life-changing message that has ever been revealed. It opens the door to salvation and a transformed, fulfilling life—but the process of discipleship is an ongoing battle. It can truly be described as fighting the good fight (2 Tim 4:7).

From early on in my pastoral counseling career, I had a sense that the best therapy was really kind of an "advanced discipleship." To live our best life in this world, there are some battles we simply must win to see the kind of fruit most of us long for in our lives. Each chapter in this study gives us a bird's-eye view of one of those "necessary victories." It is my hope to illustrate and make clear what those skirmishes are and how we can stay in the battle and tolerate the discomfort it creates. From my experience, if we keep asking, seeking, and knocking, God will provide a breakthrough if we persevere (Matt 7:7–11).

The gospel reminds us that God has taken care of our sin/guilt/death problem, so now we are free to take on the adventure of learning to live a life of courageous, adventurous faith. It is on that road that life really gets good. Thanks for being willing to come join us. Remember, there is a way!

A Biblical Model for the Trek

All counselors develop a style or model they use to help people get from the "as is" to the "stated goals." Through the years the concepts I have relied upon most are found in John 14–16. On the last night before Jesus was crucified, he spent an unforgettable teaching time with his disciples. To say this was the best group counseling session ever would be quite an understatement. It was here that Jesus referred them to their next Counselor since there would come a time when he would no longer be with them bodily. This Counselor (or *Paraclete* in the Greek language) is one of the most intriguing figures we find in Scripture.

It becomes clear as one studies John's Gospel that Jesus is speaking of the coming of the Holy Spirit—the one who lives in us and provides help for us as we begin our adventure of faith. Much has been written about the Spirit's role in our lives, but for this study, we will focus more on a description of how the Spirit counsels us as we work to become the person God created us to be.

As you study John's Gospel, you will find that there are three major roles that the Counselor plays as the Spirit helps us navigate the way that leads to life.

1. The Paraclete helps, aids, advocates, and comforts (John 14:16).

2. The Counselor guides us into all truth (John 15:26; 16:13).

3. The Spirit convicts us of sin (John 16:8).

As you read John 14–16, what things stand out to you about the one Jesus will send to assist us on our spiritual trek? It is fascinating to see how this trio of characteristics parallels with what we have come to know about good therapy or good discipleship. Good outcomes in the counseling field are almost always accompanied by what is called a good therapeutic alliance. This refers to the advocacy that gets created when a counselor creates a trusting, empathic environment. Think about someone who has walked beside you through a challenging time in life. This is someone that you know is for you, and they see the best in you. This is the person who has your back, and you sense that they genuinely like you. This quality of the Spirit's work reminds me of the apostle Paul's perfect description of God in Rom 8:31–39 when he says nothing can separate us from the love of God who is "for us."

The second attribute of the Paraclete involves guidance into truth. How important is this in a day and time when there are so many conflicting views on what qualifies as truth? We benefit from guides in many different aspects of life. The tour guide gives you insider information on the significance of what you are seeing. The fishing guide helps you pick a spot where you are most likely to land a big one. The park guide leads you to the most scenic spots, where you might even get to see a bear. How much more valuable to have someone who will guide you into truth about yourself, about others, about God, and about life itself? The journey we will face in this life is filled with ambiguity and can feel like uncharted waters, but spiritual direction is a gift that God is willing to provide if we latch onto the courage required to move from bondage to freedom.

The third component of this triad is the "convicting" skill of the Paraclete. Becoming a disciple of Jesus does have its moments of confrontation. Jesus is filled with both grace and truth, and the truth can be hard to swallow sometimes. This facet of the Spirit's work is seen more clearly in the work of the prophets. In the Old Testament, God would raise up people who were gifted at speaking the truth, especially to people who did not want to hear it. When destructive lifestyles become the norm and common sense is twisted by a culture, God will find a way to step in and try to correct the trajectory of that individual or that nation. Have you ever heard the old saying, "we don't know what we don't know"? Some of the things that we desperately need to see to make necessary changes are outside the realm of our consciousness. Psalm 139:23–24 encourages us to ask God to reveal our anxious thoughts and our offensive ways. The Lord is willing to "lead [us] in the way everlasting."

As an easy way to remember these three primary goals of the Spirit and how we can embody these qualities as we disciple others, I like to think of it as

- Joining
- Journeying
- Jousting (this third "J" word was the idea of an awesome colleague, Phil Drake)

If we put all this together, what we find is the Spirit is continually luring and aiming us toward the best possible choices and direction. It is the desire of the Paraclete to provide courage and support that we might stay on this road even though this path is marked by the exposing light of God's truth. This is no easy task since the "Son-light" illuminates all our smudges and blemishes. Jesus made it clear that our sinful nature "prefers the darkness" (John 3:19). Like Adam and Eve of old, we are very good at finding hiding places and we are still in the business of manufacturing state-of-the-art fig leaves. Without an Advocate, it is difficult to imagine exposing our bruised souls before a holy God or maintaining a courageous openness in an unsafe world. Both aspects of our journey require a Paraclete.

Here are some summary statements to help you put all this together in a way that hopefully sets you on course not only to journey well yourself, but also to help others along the way.

1. There is a way that leads to life.

2. The Holy Spirit is keenly interested in teaching us this "way" and is, in fact, constantly aiming us in that direction.

3. This way requires light, truth, and revelation to be reached.

4. Our lives are veiled by varying degrees of darkness depending on our context and experiences. Every disappointment from our past tends to add another layer of cloud cover to restrict the light.

5. The Paraclete provides gracious advocacy so that we, as skittish souls, can tolerate the uncomfortable parts of the journey.

6. When we mature and can disciple others, we too can reflect the grace and truth of Christ to aid others on this narrow road.

PART I

The Direction of the Journey

1

The Greatest Commandment

I t makes sense that a discussion of our life journey would
start with what Jesus called "the greatest commandment"
(Matt 22:37–38). To love God with all our heart, soul, mind,
and strength is deemed the most important directional signal
we have. These words of Jesus become the ultimate "North Star
principle" in Scripture.

If you have ever stargazed, you will notice that everything
we see in the heavens appears to rotate because the earth is spinning. Therefore, if you look at the stars during different seasons,
you will notice that things have appeared to move. However, the
North Star, Polaris, remains a constant. It is a reliable guide that
steers us perfectly to the north. It happens this way because Polaris is located almost perfectly at the north celestial pole, thus the
entire northern sky appears to rotate around it. Before the days
of GPS, and even before compasses, people were able to get their
bearings at night because they discovered the North Star. When all
else appears to be swirling around us, this star anchors our sense
of direction. So it is with this great command. To understand it
and be committed to obeying it will be a crucial part of staying on
course with where God wants to take us.

Loving God may seem like a simple enough thing, but experience has taught me that each of us has much to explore in this first, and most important, directional step. So, without overthinking it, take a moment to record some of your gut level responses to the question, "how do you envision God and what kind of feelings does that vision create?"

God's invisibility creates a challenge for all of us as we strive to determine the true nature of the Creator. The Bible helps because it provides dozens of different names and characteristics of God. Through the centuries, artists have attempted to capture images of God which might include a brilliant light, a throne room, a lion, or a lamb.

Our efforts to see God clearly are most enhanced by the clear statements that are made about Jesus. Colossians 1:15 states, "The Son is the image of the invisible God." Hebrews 1:3 makes a profound statement when it says, "The Son is the radiance of God's glory and the exact representation of his being." Jesus himself tops it all off in an exchange with Philip in John 14:9 where he asserts, "Anyone who has seen me has seen the Father."

We will have more to say about the crucial role that Jesus plays in our accurate understanding of God, but it is also important to note that Jesus is also invisible to us in this season of human history. We can read about him and be guided by his Spirit, but since he is no longer with us in bodily form, we are still confronted with the dilemmas that can be created by invisibility. People have very different images of what Christ is like. Invisibility requires us to use our skills of projection to create an image of God and Christ. This is where we can stumble into all kinds of difficulties. To illustrate this dilemma, I want to access the first of a series of psychological concepts that we will examine in this study.

Object Relations Theory

This theory is constructed around the idea that in our development as human beings we are constantly "taking in" our world around us. The technical term for this absorbing of our environment is "introjection." Over time the things we take in, swallow whole, absorb, or introject begin to shape our sense of internal reality. Some of the things we take in are very healthy, such as loving parents, encouraging friends, educational experiences, and fun hobbies. But the mind, especially when we are young, also absorbs unhealthy and traumatic things like abuse, neglect, the death of a loved one, and destructive things that come across our electronic screens.

Our internal realities are very different based on our experiences, and what we introject we also tend to project. Like a movie projector on the screen, our mind can overlay reality with our own personal internal reality. There are hundreds of illustrations we could use to describe how this plays out in our daily lives. In our world of racial unrest, does your heart feel more compassion for the police officers striving to keep peace or those who are emotionally distraught because of the injustice they have suffered? It probably depends on your life experience and your sense of reality as one strives to determine the truth about what is really happening.

To some degree, the world of conspiracy theories can be explained by object relations theory. What can seem outlandish to the general population can make perfect sense if one's internal reality is skewed just a bit.

Now, think about this when it comes to what we believe about God. Does this theory we are discussing help you understand why we have so many different religions and so many different denominations within Christianity? Does it help you grasp why we have so many struggles to stay unified even in our own local church? All this spiritual confusion has even led some to believe that human beings have totally made up the idea of a God because our image seems to come from within us.

However, the Bible is clear that there is a "true and living God." There is substantial evidence to convince us of this, and it seems that part of our great mission and journey is to dig for the truth about who God is. It will be very difficult to love the Lord with all our hearts if we do not see accurately. We find from the earliest pages of the Bible that our spiritual enemy is masterful at twisting the facts about our Creator. The serpent went right for the jugular when he planted seeds of doubt about the absolute perfection of God. We have struggled ever since.

As a contemporary example of the power of our broken internal reality, take a moment to think about the word "father." This is one term used to describe God. Jesus himself used it often. But when you think about the word "father," what kinds of images come to your mind? How many kinds of fathers are there on this planet? There are faithful ones, kind ones, alcoholic ones, absent ones, loving ones, abusive ones, doting ones, dead ones, and the list goes on and on. I have seen firsthand how the qualities of our earthly fathers can get projected onto God in ways that make it easy or hard to get a bead on what our heavenly Father is really like, and this is just one of many things we are forced to determine about an invisible God.

I grew up in a very conservative church environment, and although I benefitted in many ways from the things I was taught, I have also spent a lifetime finding it difficult to deeply love God. I find it quite easy to fear God, to want to please, and to be dutiful toward the Lord. I introjected plenty of sermons and lessons that led me to an image of God where those behaviors made perfect sense. But my ability to love God has not been my default setting.

I love observing people, and one thing I have observed repeatedly is that I am not alone in this struggle to find my stride with the greatest commandment. Even though the Bible is filled with descriptions of God that should make it easy for us to adore, there is something within us that does not naturally love God with all our heart, mind, soul, and strength. Have you absorbed ideas and concepts over the course of your lifetime that have limited or blocked your love for God?

Learning to Love God

The trek toward this crucial North Star begins with a prayer. Human effort alone will not get us to this destination. We need the help of the Paraclete. The prayer might be "Lord, help me see you as you really are," or "Lord, help me experience the joy that comes from the salvation you have provided," or simply, "Lord, I need your help in order to love you in the way you have asked of me." Feel free to write your prayer in your favorite journal as you evaluate the importance of learning to love God well.

I want to highlight two key elements that I have seen be highly beneficial to those who are committed to loving God. First is applying what we have learned about introjection. There is great value in "taking in" accurate information and experiences about the true nature of God. Second is developing an answer to our nagging questions about the suffering we see all around us. There is no greater threat to our ability to love God. If we see God as responsible for the condition of our world, love for the Lord becomes exponentially more difficult. Let's take these two things one at a time.

This may seem like a strange place to start but hang in there with me for a moment. In John 6:53, Jesus says, "Unless you eat the flesh of the Son of Man and drink his blood, you have no life in you." His audience back then had the same sort of difficulty we have in trying to understand what Jesus meant. We know his words were symbolic. He was not suggesting something that one might see in a horror movie. And this is not the first time in the Bible that someone was commanded to eat something that one would not typically eat. Ezekiel, an Old Testament prophet, was commanded to eat a scroll.

We still use language today that conveys the same concepts. Maybe you have heard someone say, "That book was so good, I just devoured it." It is about taking it in. It is about consuming the words, concepts, and ideas. It is a fascinating connection with the definition of introjection we have already discussed. It involves our life experiences and what we absorb or digest, specifically, the things we experience over and over, until they become a shaping force in our perception of reality. When Jesus came, he very much wanted us to know the truth about our Creator. In fact, Jesus is God in human form. So, when he says to symbolically eat his flesh and drink his blood, he wants us to take him in—to introject him in a way that begins to shape our reality in the way of truth.

In the Sermon on the Mount, Jesus teaches us that "if your eyes are healthy, your whole body is full of light, but if your eyes are unhealthy, your whole body will be full of darkness" (Matt 6:22–23). When it comes to our ability to see God accurately, we have our best chance at twenty-twenty vision when we are "taking in Christ."

Obviously, reading Scripture is one way to do this. I have also found that one does well to look for contemporary sources of truth that aid you in seeing God accurately. I see him best through the writings of Timothy Keller, or a media effort such as Angel Studio's *The Chosen*. They capture the attractive, heroic nature of Jesus in a magnificent way. For those of you who have a harsh image of God, it is wise to purposely study his love, his grace, and his mercy. Dane Ortlund's book *Gentle and Lowly* is an incredibly inspiring work about the heart of Christ. Take it all in and begin to see the irresistible character of the true and living God.

Other healthy introjection opportunities might include the entire enriching field of spiritual practices and disciplines. The writing of people like Dallas Willard or David Benner are designed to develop life patterns that correct our perceptions and help us have a vision of God that is irresistible.

I have become convinced if we could spend just a few seconds with our glorious God, without our distortions, there would be no turning back from what we encountered and we would long for more. I would compare this to the encounter the two disciples had when they walked with the risen Christ on the road to Emmaus (Luke 24:13–35). There was a reason their "hearts burned within them" as Jesus opened the Scriptures to them. In that moment, they saw him as he really is. What kinds of things are you willing to do to introject true information about God, so that your projections are an accurate portrayal of a God who is magnetic to move toward with all your heart?

The second part of learning to love God involves wrestling with the age-old question of "how does a good and loving God allow the degree of suffering we see in this broken world?" From my observation, if we see God as ultimately responsible for all the pain we see around us, it will be very hard to fully draw near and see God as glorious.

Obviously, volumes have been written on this subject by men and women much smarter than me. I will not be able to satisfactorily answer all your questions on this challenging subject, but I do want to plant a few seeds that I hope will be helpful as you do your work in this key area of the spiritual journey.

First, there are many "wills" in the universe. God has a will. Satan has a will. Mother Theresa had a will, and Adolf Hitler had a will. You and I have a will. When we look out over our world today, what we see is the conglomeration of all those wills—past and present. We could fuss about why God allowed other beings to have the level of freedom we have, but it is obvious when you think things through that love requires a freedom of will. Things like obedience or submission might be possible by way of control or restriction, but love requires a will, a free choice. God clearly decided that love was worth the risk of a rebellion.

Second, God grieves with us about the condition of our world. Because God is holy and perfect, sin requires consequences, but the Bible is clear that God finds no pleasure in the cascading repercussions of the misuse of our wills (Ezek18:30–32). Correction and judgment are necessary aspects of God's response to our corrupt world, but those things are not his heart. Speak with any loving parent, and they will tell you that they are grieved when they must be punitive with their children and long for getting passed that so loving reconciliation can be restored.

Third, God is not king of this world, yet. I realize this is a controversial statement but let me explain. The Bible clearly teaches that God is sovereign over the whole universe. No one who trusts Scripture as God's inspired word could dispute that. God's ultimate destination will be reached. However, there is much evidence that the suffering we see in this world is a result of where we are in history. There are reasons why Satan is referred to as the "prince of this world" (John 12:31). There is a reason why Jesus prayed in the model prayer. "Father . . . your will be done, on earth as it is in heaven" (Matt 6:9-13) It seems evident the Father's will is not done on earth as it is in heaven, thus the need for that prayer. Second Peter 3:9 says the Lord wants everyone to come to repentance, but clearly that has not happened. We get a glimpse at the twisted nature of our planet when we realize that Jesus—God in human form—came into this world, and we crucified him. There will be a considerably more favorable reception for one the Bible calls the antichrist, Satan incarnate (Rev 13:1–4). One of my mental images when it comes to suffering is the comparison of our planet to a giant aircraft. Jesus is the only one who can successfully pilot it, and we threw him off the plane. No wonder, there is havoc all around us.

Fourth, this world has dealt with more than its share of tribulation. But, at the end of all that suffering and confusion, God the King will arrive. When the Lord fully takes the throne of this world and makes all things new, the suffering disappears. There will be no more tears, no more death, no more curse, no more anxiety. Those who place their trust in God will get to see truth in all its glory, with no more veil, no more deception, no more doubts, and all our questions will quickly evaporate as we experience a brand-new chapter in history. I often wonder what our love for God will feel like then!

Based on what you have read in this chapter, what areas do you feel you need to focus upon to move forward with a greater ability to love God with all your heart, soul, mind, and strength?

Case Study—Jack

Several years ago, a young man in his mid-twenties walked into my office. All I knew from his intake form was that he served a church as an associate pastor, and he was struggling with some depressive feelings. As Jack settled into his chair, the things I noticed most were a bit of an unkempt look and his hoodie pulled up around his head, almost like he was hiding from someone.

I began as I often do with an expression of my appreciation of his courage for a willingness to come and talk about some important things in his life. As his story unfolded, I found that he was rather miserable serving in a church under the leadership of a senior pastor who was difficult to respect and who had a rather oppressive, critical style. The bigger issue, however, was that Jack had experienced a moral failure. Given the sensitivity of his conscience, the guilt and shame were eating him up. He had confessed this to his wife, and she had graciously decided to stay with him and work through the fallout his sin had created. There was much trust to rebuild.

Some years after our counseling work together, Jack was reflecting with me about that first session we had together. He told me that as he shared his story with me, he was not able to look at me in that moment, and he braced himself for the judgmental response he anticipated from me—a clear description of his projection. He said what happened instead was I spoke to him in a compassionate tone and said, "That must have really been hard." It was enough of a surprise that he lifted his head, and that was the beginning of an incredible trek to a better spiritual and emotional place.

Some of Jack's introjections were unhealthy. He described his dad as distant and unskilled at being a father. For many men, what they do not do well, they tend to avoid. The avoidance of his father coupled with a less-than-healthy father figure in his senior pastor had a hefty impact on Jack's image of God. At the core, Jack was angry with God and had numerous questions and doubts that riddled his thinking. As you might imagine, having that internal struggle and being in a ministry position created quite the civil war at the soul level.

After some months of creating an emotionally safe environment to talk honestly about his doubts and struggles, something rather amazing happened. Jack and his wife found out they were expecting their first child. I wondered what impact this may have on Jack's relationship with God, but it soon became evident that the thought of being a father and doing it well renewed his faith, and as the months of the pregnancy rolled by, his anticipation surged.

Then, the complications developed. His wife's blood pressure rose and required her to be on bed rest. The following week an ultrasound revealed some serious medical concerns for the child. The doctors braced the young couple for the worst. At that point, my own questions and doubts arose. Why Lord? Why this couple? Why this young man who wants to trust you, but finds it so difficult, who already feels his life is under a curse? I tried to prepare myself for the next time I would see him, where I anticipated that his anger and confusion would reign.

But what I received instead was an incredible view into the amazing ability of the Holy Spirit to comfort his people. Jack responded, "My primary thought has been how much I want this little girl. Even if she is born with problems, I just want her to live." He went on to say that God had impressed on his heart an important parallel regarding the way the Lord feels about us. "I am full of serious imperfections, but maybe, just maybe, God wants me just as much as I want this daughter of mine." That moment in Jack's journey opened the door for him to begin to love God with all his heart, and many things began to fall into place for him.

His child was born, and although there were a few health issues, she is now a healthy teenager and the apple of her mom and dad's eye. Back then, Jack stepped out of ministry for a time to continue trying to live a more authentic life. He tried a few things career wise, but ultimately decided to go to graduate school, and is now a skilled therapist helping many people find their way just as he found his. To be around him, you know that he is living out his faith in a God he loves.

I am very aware that every story does not have as happy an ending as this one. But I hope this case illustrates for all of us that removing the obstacles and getting an accurate view of God is the key to being able to love the Lord. Remember, if we were able to see accurately for just a few seconds, God would be the hero we would follow anywhere for the rest of our days. Jack and I both agree that loving God is where the journey begins to get good. Take time to share any additional personal reflections you have experienced as you have read this first chapter.

2

Teachability

L et us begin this chapter with a simple, yet profound question. How much do you think God has to teach you? Take a few minutes to reflect upon this and record your thoughts. When you ponder the fact that God is omniscient and that he desires to give wisdom (Jas 1:5), it makes perfect sense that we would all have a fierce appetite for what God offers. However, when you look at our world, it certainly has not turned out that way. So, the concept of teachability becomes the second key ingredient of our spiritual journey and our ability to discover "the way."

Being teachable is crucial to our spiritual trek because many of the things God desires to teach us are going to be different and unexpected. The Old Testament makes it clear that God's ways and our ways are different (Isa 55:8). Those who make the most of their spiritual journey in this life tend to have the mindset of a lifelong learner. They have enough humility to realize that everyone has blind spots and as a result, they just might be wrong about a few things that they hold dear. It is the person who embraces the commitment to keep asking, seeking, and knocking (Matt 7:7) that finds the spiritual treasures along the way.

Have you ever noticed as you have read the Gospels just how many inaccurate assumptions were prominent among the religious people of Jesus's day?

- Nothing good can come out of Nazareth.

- The Messiah will free us from Roman oppression.

- Healing someone on the Sabbath means you cannot be from God.

- God despises gentiles, tax collectors, and sinners.

- Suffering is directly connected to some sin we have committed.

We do well to remember that our generation is likely to be wrong about some things too. However, when you listen to those on either end of the conservative/liberal continuum, you would think they are absolutely 100 percent correct on everything they assert. They seem so certain and unyielding in their position.

I find it interesting that the Bible consistently points us to maturity. That makes sense, right? We want to grow up and develop into experienced, complete people. Yet, along with that goal, Jesus tells us that we "will never enter the kingdom of heaven" unless we become like little children (Matt 18:3). It is ironic that Jesus would teach us to be both mature, yet childlike.

The context of the Matt 18 passage involved Jesus's disciples asking a question about who would be greatest in the kingdom of heaven. This sense of "who is the greatest?" would come up more than once among the disciples. Adults are sensitive to power and control. It does not take much to activate our competitiveness, especially if we are convinced our way is the best.

Jesus often made the point that in his kingdom, it is the humble and lowly person that is exalted. So, when he speaks of childlikeness, he is talking about humility, teachability, and that eagerness to learn—not to take charge and be oppressive with our position. Have you been around a curious child lately? It is often one question after another, and at their best, children are like little sponges, soaking up whatever they can learn about how the world works. It will serve us best on our journey with Jesus to cultivate that attitude. He has much to teach and show us, and from my experience, it is very difficult to predict how Jesus will lead us from where we are to where he wants us to be.

When you look back over your Christian life, what would you identify as something you were wrong about that you now see more clearly? Consider the old saying, "we don't know what we don't know." Can you think of a pivotal time when God rolled back the curtain and helped you see something that you were once blind to?

The Holding Environment

In the counseling field, we sometimes think of therapy as a container or a "holding environment," where people can feel emotionally safe enough to unpack their thoughts and feelings without the fear of punishment or judgment. The word picture that comes to mind for me is an incubator. When I was in elementary school, one of my classmates lived on a farm and raised chickens. We also had a teacher who loved giving us firsthand experience of how life works. So, she brought an incubator, and the student brought some eggs from the farm. We put the eggs in the temperature-regulated box, and we were told that after twenty-one days or so, baby chickens may come out. Well, I had never seen that before, so I was fascinated by this classroom lesson. Every day we would check the thermometer to make sure the incubator was the ideal temperature for the eggs, and sure enough, one day we began to see movement and cracks began to develop in the shells, and ultimately, out came baby chicks. Amazing!

However, as cool as that was, it does not compare with what I get to see as a counselor. There is nothing quite like joining and journeying with a client, and getting to hear them say something like "I have never shared this with anyone before, but I want to let you know that . . ." When people feel enough trust to disclose things that have been heavy to carry or have caused them shame, that creates a different kind of shell-breaking experience.

To watch the hard soil be cracked open and tilled like that is truly a "sacred ground" experience.

The beauty of this concept is that it does not just happen in a counseling office. I have observed it in a well-delivered sermon or a small group setting. People have felt this kind of powerful transformation in a twelve-step group or in a family meeting between a parent and a teen. The primary active ingredients are healthy amounts of "grace and truth." From my experience, human beings will not open their hearts and be teachable if they do not feel emotionally safe to do so. We have too many defense mechanisms at our disposal (more about this in chapter 4), and we are typically not willing to remove our armor and experience vulnerability unless we trust. A gracious environment is required if we want people to be honest, and honesty is required because as Jesus said, it is "truth that sets us free" (John 8:32).

I think there is a reason why John 1:14 has always been my favorite description of Jesus. "The Word became flesh and made his dwelling among us. We have seen his glory, the glory of the one and only Son who came from the Father, full of grace and truth." In real-life pastoral situations such as Jesus's encounter with the woman accused of adultery, he modeled for us that the "neither do I condemn you" part of the message precedes the "go and leave your life of sin" part (John 8:1–11). Grace and truth are both required.

What settings do you have in your life where you feel emotionally safe enough to share the most vulnerable parts of who you are? If you are not able to identify an incubator-type environment for yourself, I encourage you to prayerfully be on the lookout for that family member, friend, counselor, small group, Sunday school class, or church that cares about you enough to model that safe space God provides where we can "speak the truth in love" (Eph 4:15) to one another.

Can You Handle the Truth?

Teachability is all about embracing the truth, but most would agree that there are times when the truth is hard to handle, especially the kind of truth that threatens and exposes us in a painful way. In some ways, the Christian life magnifies the challenge of facing hard truths. Here we are serving a perfect God, all the while knowing that we are very imperfect people. We want to please God and conform to God's guidance, but we never measure up. So, how do we reconcile this uncomfortable truth? I know of no greater answer to this question than a thorough look at Matt 23. Let us dig in.

I want to begin at the end of the chapter, where Jesus illustrates the importance of grace and his ability to create the holding environment or "incubator" for his people. Carefully read these words: "Jerusalem, Jerusalem, you who kill the prophets and stone those sent to you, how often I have longed to gather your children together, as a hen gathers her chicks under her wings, and you were not willing" (Matt 23:37). In Luke's Palm Sunday account, he adds that Jesus wept over Jerusalem as he entered it because he knew its days were numbered before destruction would come.

This is an amazing observation point to gaze at God's grace. The city had a history of killing and stoning those whom God had sent. Why? Because the role of God's prophets and other messengers was to speak truth. As we have already mentioned, part of the Paraclete's role is to speak convicting truth. But, even with Jerusalem's violent, abusive reputation, Jesus wept over them and wanted to embrace and protect them. It is hard to imagine a more powerful illustration of God's grace than what we see here—other than what would happen a few days later when Jesus gave his life for us on the cross.

It is safe to say that regardless of our past, no matter how messy our lives, the Lord wants to create a safe place for us to be honest about who we are and what we have done. The invitation is to lay down all the defensiveness and self-protection, and to face the hard truth about our weaknesses, our imperfections, and our sins. God has solutions to all those things, if we are willing to be taught and guided into all truth. We stay on course with the Spirit of God when we can be honest and teachable.

Sadly, it did not end that way for most of the religious leaders of Jesus's day. Matthew 23 is marked by the words like "woe" and "hypocrites." We still hear the concept of hypocrisy these days when people talk about religious folks who do not "walk the talk." In Jesus's time, this word hypocrite literally meant "wearing a mask." We still live in a world of image management, where our presentation of ourselves does not always match up with what life is like behind closed doors. The real danger of this masked lifestyle is that over time it can develop into what is sometimes referred to as a "false self." A person can live a lie for so long that they begin to believe it, and reality is altered in ways that are highly resistant to the Spirit's efforts to penetrate.

This was the plight of the Pharisees. They had become the epitome of a legalistic pride that was very destructive for them and the people they tried to convert to their form of religion. In many ways, the religious leaders of Jesus's day represent the trappings of religion for all generations. Let's take a closer look and see if we can expose the trap, so that we do not end up in a place of hard-hearted refusal to accept the truth and thus lose our teachability.

My attempt to summarize the key message of Matt 23 looks like this:

- God is perfect in every way.

- God's law is also perfect and designed to guide us into all truth.

- We are flawed people and despite our best efforts we cannot measure up to the law.

- Falling short of God's standard is uncomfortable for us and creates guilt or shame.

This discomfort leads people to try to reduce the pain by one of several reactions. We can convince ourselves that God (and his law) does not exist. We can alter God in our mind in ways that help us feel better about ourselves. We can deceive ourselves into believing we really are keeping God's law. We can convince ourselves that at least we are better than other people.

As I reflect on Matt 23, I have a deepening understanding of Jesus's grief. His gospel was the real solution to the Pharisees' dilemma. He wanted them to know that he had a way to save them. His sacrifice was the answer to their flawed nature. They could come to him, open and vulnerable, and experience his grace, but they were trapped in their defensiveness. They were wearing masks that were designed to convince themselves and others that they were without fault and exemplary in every way. They polished the outside of the cup and they whitewashed the outside of the tomb—but it was only a veneer, a thin pathetic defense against the truth about their arrogant hearts. This was the message the prophets brought to them, the message that John the Baptist had brought to them, and finally that Jesus had brought to them. But they persecuted and killed the "voices of truth" because they could not handle the truth. The holding environment was offered to them, a message of great grace and safety to unpack their sinful baggage, but they were committed to their defensive efforts, and it ultimately led them to crucify the One that was sent to be their Messiah.

It is interesting to study the biblical language of defensiveness. One sees terms like hard-hearted, calloused, and stiff-necked. The cost of these tactics ultimately led to a life which Jesus described as "hearing but never understanding, seeing but never perceiving" (Matt 13:14). What a sad thing to lose our ears to hear and our eyes to see.

This religious struggle still exists today. Sometimes people are hesitant to go to church because they can feel judged by a "holier-than-thou" attitude. Sometimes people see the Christian faith as just another set of rules they cannot keep, so what is the use? Is there something about God or God's people that has tended to keep you from seeing the church as a "holding environment" that invites you to shed your defenses and just be real about your struggles?

It is only in the context of a gracious environment that our teachability reaches its full potential. When you no longer fear condemnation or the other shoe that could drop at any moment, the future becomes less threatening and the adventure of discovering what God has for you is welcomed rather than held at arm's length. The good news is that grace abounds. God has much to share with us and if we are courageous enough to walk with God into the unknown, a journey like no other awaits us. Do not allow your fears to keep you from the course the Lord has laid out for you. Remember what we studied in chapter 1. He deeply loves us and is for us in every way.

Case Study—Ben

When I met Ben, he was in his early thirties. He had been out on his own, but for financial reasons needed to move back home with his parents. He was between jobs and had become quite depressed. The early months of therapy with Ben were excruciating. I remember how much powerlessness I felt as a counselor because Ben was so down on himself and would tend to have a "yes, but . . ." answer to anything that seemed like it might be a step forward. In his mind, there always seemed to be a reason why things would not work for him.

Now before you draw too many conclusions about Ben, realize that he was a college graduate and had a master's degree in music. His original sense of calling was to be a worship pastor. He had one opportunity to work in a small church that barely paid him, and that had not gone very well. So, he felt like all that work, all that training, all those hopes, were a waste.

He had also very much hoped to be married by now, and have a family of his own, but instead here he was feeling embarrassed being back home with his parents yet lacking the energy to push toward his dreams. Ben's mindset had become "I've given my best, and it is not good enough. God does not seem to want to help me, so since life does not offer much to me, I am likely to be miserable for the rest of my days." Hopelessness and despair had found a nesting place in his heart and mind, and Ben struggled to accept other interpretations of what might be going on in his life.

I will never forget one session where Ben's parents asked if they could join us. They were concerned about him, and his dad was really pushing him to get a job. I looked at his parents and said, "Understandably, you are anxious about Ben finding a direction for his life, but it is important for you to know he is battling something much more basic. He is trying to decide whether he wants to live or not." You could have heard a pin drop at that point. But it was kind of a turning point for us. Ben and his family began to realize we were looking for a reason to keep fighting and not give in to the unspeakable despair that had crept in and begun to haunt him.

It was a slow arduous journey, but my alliance with Ben grew strong. He knew that I cared deeply for him and that I wanted to lend him my hope until he had more of his own. That incubator environment earned me the right to challenge some of his conclusions about how he ended up unemployed. I remember noting for him that his reserved, melancholy personality might not be the best match for a worship leader in today's culture. Ben was very musically talented, but I had a sense he would have fit better in a different era of history. In our current church world of charisma, stage presence, and high energy, Ben appeared to run low in those qualities most churches seem to be seeking.

It was very hard for Ben to hear that he may have misjudged some things regarding the kind of match he would be for our day and time. But, to his credit, he took those concepts and chewed on them. As we continued meeting weekly for several months, I noticed that Ben often spoke of working on his computer. I am not very techie, so it does not take much to impress me, but it seemed to me he was very knowledgeable and enjoyed talking about technology.

I asked him if he had ever considered going back to school and getting some formal training in that field. He had not, because in his state of mind, it would just be another risk of failure. But he did investigate what was offered at the local community college. He ended up taking a class or two and excelled. Professors encouraged him because they saw his potential, and over the next eighteen months or so, he got an associate's degree.

Momentum began to build. He had been working part-time just to make some money, but after getting the degree, he got a job in his new field, and again was doing outstanding work. He was now earning enough to feel he could enter a more normal life. However, now being in his mid-thirties, Ben lamented the time he felt he had lost. We grieved that together, but I reminded him that it was best to stay focused on what we could do rather than being stuck on something out of our control.

As life opportunities began to open for him, he decided to try his hand at computer dating. He met a young woman his age who had spent several years as part of an evangelistic ministry team. She is a musician and currently uses those skills to serve in her local church along with teaching piano to young students in her home. Ben could hardly believe all these good things were happening to him. One day we were reflecting on all that he had been through, and I made the observation that he had always felt that his training in music was a waste. However, his new girlfriend had indicated that one of the things that caused her to respond to him in their early conversations online was that he was a music major in college and seminary. Ben broke down and began weeping as that insight took root.

To make a long story short, they dated, got engaged, and married. A year or two later, Ben contacted me to let me know he was going to be a father. I still smile when I think about Ben. I also wonder what might have become of him if he had not allowed the hard soil of his disappointments to be tilled up and cultivated by the God who certainly has the capacity to work all things together for good for those who love him and are called according to his purpose (Rom 8:28). Can you remember a time when God surprised you with a breakthrough when you had just about given up?

3

The Uniqueness of Your Journey

I n the first two chapters, we focused upon the direction of the journey and our teachability along the way. This concluding chapter of part one will turn our attention to the fact that no two people will have the exact same journey. It is not a "one-size-fits-all" endeavor. We can take comfort in knowing that we will travel alongside others and have common ground at times, but be assured there will also be seasons where we must be secure enough to take a Spirit-led path that not everyone else will fully understand.

This chapter is all about the formation of our unique identity and becoming who God created us to be. As we enter a discussion about identity formation, we will be considering questions like these:

- Do you believe God has a plan for your life?
- Did God create you with a specific purpose in mind?
- How can you truly know the will of God for your kingdom service?
- How does God communicate a unique direction for your life?

These kinds of questions can leave our heads spinning, and in a broken world, it is often hard to get clear answers to them; but there are some principles that I feel certain can assist us in finding that "road that leads to life" (Matt 7:14). From my observation, the real pay dirt of this discussion about identity is found in paying attention to one's will. Solid identity formation involves a growing understanding of God's will, my will, and the will of others. In a fractured world, these three wills are like a complex intersection where car crashes are common. The Bible has much to say about how to bring balance to these three important voices that we all have in our heads. As we dig into this discussion about the balance of wills, let's start at the beginning.

Back to Creation

From the first chapter of Genesis, we get a clear snapshot that our God is a creative Creator. No matter where we look, we see splendor and variety that is really beyond description. Visit any planetarium, botanical garden, aquarium, aviary, or zoo and you will sense color, texture, and complexity that can awe and overwhelm.

After creating stars, plants, and animals, God created human beings, and that was even more amazing because we were created in God's image. When you look closely at the language of Gen 1, it is evident that there is an element of royalty for us as humans. Adam and Eve were created in God's image to rule (Gen 1:26). In David's commentary on this passage in Ps 8, he states that we are to be rulers and that God crowned us with glory and honor. We are also told that at the end of this age, when Christ reigns in the fullness of his kingdom, we will reign with him.

Obviously, since our world was broken by sin, we do not feel much like royalty, but if we can filter out all the esteem-damaging messages this world throws at us, it is still true that your life is a kind of personal kingdom where each of us have the freedom to build an identity. We make hundreds of decisions every day that reflect the fact that we have a will and a small territory where we have both the freedom and the responsibility to call the shots. One of my favorite pastors to listen to these days is Trevor Barton at The Creek Church in London, Kentucky. He reminded me in a recent sermon that the first recorded words from God to man in Scripture were "you are free" (Gen 2:16).

It is also evident from the creation account that there was to be a certain order to this freedom. The Creator is the king of the universe. The humans (Adam and Eve) were delegated a limited rule as God's representatives on the planet over the created garden of Eden. So, the order looked like this:

- God

- Humans

- Earth

However, there was a third "will" that entered the picture. God had a will, Adam and Eve had a will, and the serpent had a will. We know how that ended. It would seem the enemy tempted Eve/Adam in the same way he had come to his own fall—pride and a challenge to God's established order. The pursuit of equality with God by elevating our will to the status of God's is still playing out in every human life to this very day. There was only one who prayed, "Not my will, but yours be done" and lived it out without failure.

When I hear the biblical description of Jesus as King of kings and Lord of lords, I like to think of him as King of the universe, thus having authority over all earthly nations and leaders. Colossians 1:16 remind us, "For in him were all things created: things in heaven and on earth, visible and invisible, whether thrones or power or rulers or authorities; all things have been created through him and for him." That means he is also Lord over me and you in our little personal domain, where God has given us our acreage to cultivate our sense of personhood and creativity. It is evident that God wants to empower us and set us free in this unique blend of Spirit-led personal identity. Galatians 5:1 reminds us, "It is for freedom that Christ has set us free."

Claiming our identity in Christ helps us be more intentional about the way we utilize the life he gave us. Without this clear sense of being purposely created and valued by God, we can easily fall into a twisted view that we are just one of nearly eight billion people on the planet, and that our life is random and without clear meaning. Have you taken time lately to think about God's original intention for human beings? What do you think it means to be created in God's image? What is your best guess as to why you are here?

Sun or Planet or Moon?

In a parenting class that I have taught for several years, I try to give young parents a heads-up that about half of children tend to have a compliant style, while the other half have a strong-willed personality. Compliant kids want to learn what parents want from them so they can please them. Strong-willed kids want to know what parents want so they can challenge it. It is obvious that God created and blesses both styles, and each one has its own set of strengths and weaknesses. My wife and I have two daughters, one more compliant and one more strong-willed, and it has been quite an adventure to see how these two different temperaments played out over time. When it comes to our spiritual journey, both styles have a specific challenge.

Once again, I would like to turn to a word picture from the field of astronomy. One of the differences between a planet and a moon is the nature of its orbit. A planet revolves around the sun, while a moon revolves around a planet. The sun is central in both location and importance to life in our little corner of the galaxy. Without it, life as we know it would not exist.

I see human beings designed by God to be more like planets. We each have an individual orbit or journey that is designed to revolve around our Creator. However, compliant people, if they are not careful, can find themselves arranging their lives around the will of other people. The Bible provides warning about falling into the trap of pleasing people more than pleasing God. External control of our lives can take many forms. It might be peer pressure, linking oneself to the current political correctness model, or creating a codependent relationship with one individual. Regardless of the form it takes, falling into the pleaser trap will cause us to act more like a moon and land us in a very complicated orbit.

In the psychology field, there is an important concept referred to as "locus of control." The word "locus" is a Latin term meaning "place." When you think about your process for making decisions, what is your control center for navigating your life? People with an external locus of control tend to get their cues from outside sources. Those who look more within themselves are said to have an internal locus of control. We will say more about God's plan for this later in the chapter.

In case you have not noticed, there will always be external sources who want to influence you or have an agenda for your life. Jesus faced a steady barrage of advice and pressure during his ministry. The devil tempted him. The religious leaders opposed his teaching. The crowds pressured him to be king. Even one of his own disciples, Peter, tried to steer him away from his appointed mission (Matt 16:22–23). But Jesus demonstrated the value and dignity given to us as human beings. We were created to be planets, not moons. We are to revolve around the will of God—revealed through the word of God and the Holy Spirit. One of Jesus's most common statements was, "I have come to do the will of my Father." That is our target, and the way to our true destination.

I tend to be a compliant person. I like keeping the rules and I feel more comfortable when people are happy with me. I suspect about half of you will be nodding your heads at this point, knowing what that feels like. I can still remember in my younger days saying yes to a few high pressures salespeople just because I wanted to please them. However, I am also tight with money, so it did not take too long to figure out that I needed to learn how to say no, even if people were disappointed. One of the first big tests I remember facing was my decision to launch into the world of pastoral counseling. I noticed early in my ministry career that most of the fruitful things that happened were in my one-on-one pastoral conversations with people. I explored the counseling field, and some doors began to open for me to gain some specialized training.

As I shared my growing sense of pastoral identity with people, I noticed some reactions were lackluster. In the early 1980s, the pastoral counseling field was still relatively young, and several of my colleagues were skeptical of anything that involved psychology. It was viewed as a secular field and fraught with dangers from a faith perspective. The torn-ness I felt was significant; however, as I continued to pray and wrestle with this decision, I sensed the Spirit was leading me toward an area of ministry specializing in pastoral counseling, even though there were some influential people who did not seem to be happy with my direction. After all these years, I am very grateful God gave me the internal strength to be more like a planet than a moon. What decisions are you facing in your life where the pressure from others is coming into play? What kind of difference will it make in your thinking if you view yourself as more of a planet than a moon?

Now, let us look at the other side of this coin. How does one's locus of control come into play for a strong-willed person? People with a strength of will rarely find it tempting to be a moon. Standing alone is not nearly as difficult for you. This quality tends to make you more of a leader than a follower. It would be a rare thing for a strong-willed person to sign up for an assertiveness training class.

The greater temptation is to be so determined to apply your will that even the will of God is left out of the equation. The strong-willed person can also be illustrated by our astronomy analogy. There was a time when it was thought that the earth was the center of the universe, and everything was revolving around us. It was not until the sixteenth century that Copernicus theorized that it was actually the sun at the center of our solar system, and the earth, like all the other planets, rotated around it.

To find the true destination that God has for us, we must remember that God's will is central, not ours. Jesus models this for us in the most inspiring of ways. His prayer in the garden of Gethsemane stands as the ultimate example. With the full weight of the crucifixion before him, he prays, "My Father, if it is possible, may this cup be taken from me. Yet not as I will, but as you will" (Matt 26:39).

Our will is an important gift from God, and he gives us amazing freedom to use it. But there will be times in our personal journey when we come to some very important "yield signs." There will be times when God asks us to do or say something that clashes with what we want. The very heart of submission is defined by our commitment of learning to keep God at the center of our world. We are created to be planets—not moons, not the sun, but planets. As you take a close look at your life, can you identify a time when you were determined to do what you wanted to do without consulting God for input? How did that work out? Can you think of a time when you yielded to God, even when it was hard for you?

God's Design for Identity Formation

As you wrestle with fascinating concepts such as God's created order, the will, our personal kingdom, God's love of variety, and being like a planet, I trust that it will help you pay more attention to your identity. This crucial concept of identity will help you get a clearer view that God has provided extensive freedom and valuable boundaries so that we can make our journey to our own unique destination. Through God's word and Spirit, we have received all we need to carve out a territory that honors God and allows us to be the person we were created to be.

The Scriptures reveal to us a way to discern good from evil, what is wise or foolish, and the kinds of things that please or sadden him. However, these principles are not always specific enough for us to know exactly what to do at each moment. For example, should I take that new job offer or stay where I am? Would I do well to give money to the beggar on the street or would I only be enabling some destructive pattern that landed him in this desperate situation? Should I try to be more like my extroverted friend and engage my neighbors more or is it okay for me to see my home as more of a sanctuary from dealing with the complexity of more people than I have the energy to manage?

The entire design of the Bible helps us see God's strategy for people—both our commonality and our uniqueness. In the Old Testament period, the focus was more on the law that God gave to Moses. From a psychological standpoint, this would be referred to as more of an external locus of control. However, it is clear from a New Testament perspective that God never intended this external locus to be the permanent strategy for his people.

One of my favorite verses that helps explain God's true design regarding the law is found in Gal 3:24. Paul describes the law as a guardian, a schoolmaster, a tutor, or literally from the Greek "a child-trainer." Every good parent learns that young children require a healthy external source to provide guidance. This is why the primary command to children in Scripture is to obey your parents. What would a child's food choices look like if we left it totally up to them? Hmm, let's see, broccoli or gummy bears? Would youngsters ever choose to be in a car seat where they are safer if it were left to them?

However, as children grow up, effective parents know that we ultimately want to provide more freedom and independence. So, little by little, we encourage them to search their own hearts for the decisions they make. As they launch into the world of adulthood, we hope that they are well on their way to becoming who God created them to be. It does not often go well if adults are too dependent and still looking to external sources to tell them what to do. Taking too many life cues from sources outside of our own core identity has led many people to those awkward and depressing seasons where life feels like a box canyon or a dead end. If that is where you find yourself, there is some work to do to get back to an open road that fits who you were created to be.

Therefore, the preferred developmental process is from external locus of control to internal. This is what we see as God was advancing humanity in the realm of faith. In the early going, the law was written on tablets of stone, but God foresaw a day when the law would be written on our hearts (Jer 31:33). The law was the "child trainer" to bring us to Christ.

It is no accident that an integral part of the new covenant was the sending of the Holy Spirit to live within us. As we learn to keep step with the Spirit (Gal 5:25), we now have a two-fold method for discerning how to navigate our way through our journey in this world. The word of God provides a great reservoir of inspired truth, and the Spirit personalizes this ancient wisdom and helps us apply it in the specific decisions we face every day. We can still get coaching and feedback from external sources like friends, family, pastors, books, etc., but for God's people, the best compass is within. As we learn to hear the Spirit's voice, we experience the greater freedom that the gospel intends.

When you think about the direction of your journey thus far, how have the Scriptures helped you select the path you are on? In what ways have you learned to pay attention to the "still small voice" (1 Kgs 19:12) of the Spirit in your decision-making process?

The Bible is filled with stories about people's journey. Some like Noah, Abraham, Moses, Esther, Ezekiel, Mary, and Paul had very specific callings upon their lives. In some ways, their lives were complicated by what God led them to do. However, if you were to ask them if they would trade anything for the nature of their personal kingdoms, I suspect the answer would be a clear "no."

Not everyone seems to have such a clear sense of calling for their lives, but it is where our ears should be attuned. As we make our hundreds of decisions every day about what we will read, what we will watch, who we will interact with, where we will spend our money, how we will cope with the stressors of life, and whether we will pray, we do well to be listening to God's word and the Holy Spirit.

At any time, God may choose to pry us out of our patterns and routines and recalibrate our course toward something to be incorporated into our personal kingdom, so that God's will can be done in our lives and our world. Whether it is big or small, I hope that we will respond with the famous words of Isaiah when he was called by God and said, "Here am I, send me!" (Isa 6:8).

Case Study—Michelle

From 2005 to 2020, I served part-time as a pastoral counselor on the staff of an urban pregnancy resource center. It has truly been a highlight of my ministry career. I have often likened it to being a cross-cultural missionary in my own backyard. I would describe our center as a pro-life ministry that was not only interested in giving young women a supportive alternative to abortion, but also building meaningful relationships with people from diverse backgrounds regardless of the choices they had made in the past. Our team just wanted to help where we could and show people the love of Christ during one of the most stressful times of their lives. This is where I met Michelle.

Michelle's family was from another country. She was in her twenties and had lived most of her life here in the states. Even though she had faced many obstacles, Michelle is bright and re-silient and had worked hard to develop her career in the medical profession. After meeting with her a few times, it seemed evident to me that she had found her calling. She was a great fit for her role and was the kind of person you could not help but like and admire. But Michelle was in trouble emotionally.

As her story unfolded, she shared that she was in love with a young man who was also from her home country. However, he was struggling to keep up with her from a developmental stand-point. She was on a good career track and was the apple of her parents' eye, while Danny was still living at his parents' home and had not gained much traction regarding his education and future work plans.

A year or so prior to my meeting Michelle, she discovered she was pregnant, and she and Danny were facing some difficult deci-sions. While they were anxious and scared about the unexpected pregnancy and knew things would be complicated, they both wanted to have the child and plan a future together.

When Michelle approached her parents about the preg-nancy, they expressed that Michelle had deeply let them down after all the years of raising her and teaching her their cultural values. It was the first time she ever saw her father shed a tear. This was an excruciating dilemma for a compliant young woman. In a desperate attempt to lessen the pain for her parents and to try to undo her actions, she pushed aside her own internal guidance from God and suggested an abortion. Michelle indicated to me that she lied to her parents that she could do this. She knew in her own heart and mind this was the last thing she wanted, but at that moment, she felt like she had to do this for her parents and felt like she had no other choice.

On the back side of her decision, Michelle experienced a very deep grief. Danny spiraled downward even more, becoming more depressed and even finding himself in some legal trouble. Michelle's parents were not big fans of her boyfriend because of his lack of ambition, but with these added problems they were seeing in him, they felt it would be disastrous for their daughter to marry Danny. In their fear and anxiety, they began to tighten their control over Michelle's life and forbade her from seeing him.

Some months later there was another young man from her culture who had shown interest in Michelle. Her family felt he would be a great match for her, so they were very supportive of this relationship and nudged Michelle in that direction. She was incredibly stuck regarding her locus of control. She wanted to please her family but knew she could not continue to allow her parents to control her life at the level they now wanted to do.

She reported growing increasingly depressed. I often tell people there is a reason the word "press" is contained in the word "depression." In the case of situational depressions, feeling boxed in or trapped is often a major contributor. Though Michelle was internally divided, she went on several dates with the young man her parents were pleased with. It had been hard for her to set effective boundaries with her parents during this season where her deflated mood left her without much energy for conflict. Things worsened when she began to realize that the young man she was now dating also had a controlling personality style. She described to me that her mom had taken her to look at wedding dresses, and as she tried one on, she became so nauseous that she nearly vomited. She shared with me it was at this point that she realized deep down she still longed for what the future would have been with Danny and their child. As much as she wanted to keep peace in her family, she knew she was making herself ill by violating the values she held at the deepest level.

Over the next several months, Michelle and I prayerfully began to look closely at every angle of this internal conflict. She used the sharp mind God had given her to consider her options. The most immediate step she felt necessary was to be honest about her feelings toward the man her parents wanted her to marry. She very respectfully made it clear that despite the discomfort and embarrassment it might cause, she could not continue the relationship, and did the hard work of disappointing both the young man and her parents. The support provided by our therapeutic relationship was extremely important during this period. When under this kind of emotional pressure, it is often important to have advocacy with a human paraclete as one is growing to learn more about trusting the Paraclete who dwells internally.

Once this immediate pressure was relieved, it provided time for Michelle to give thought to her feelings about Danny. She respected that her parents might be right in their concern about his lack of readiness to be married and keeping pace with her development as a person. She continued to meet with Danny as a friend and have conversations with him, but made it clear that he was going to have to step up and demonstrate that he was maturing and could carry his weight in a relationship with her.

Over the next several months, Michelle decided to accept a new position that would require her to move to another state. This was not an easy step for her, but it did put some geographical boundaries in place so she could continue the differentiation process from her family, and it provided Danny an opportunity to decide whether he could keep pace with Michelle's emotional and spiritual growth.

I had not heard from Michelle for a year or two after she left town, but recently she emailed my office to let me know that Danny had gotten a job and moved to the city where she was now living.

She indicated he has made significant progress since leaving some of the influences he had at home. They have been dating again for several months, both of their families have come around to give them their blessing, and they recently have gotten engaged. She asked if I would be available to be part of their wedding ceremony next year. I have had the opportunity to meet with them a couple of times when they were in town visiting family, and I could not be happier for the good work they have done and the reward they are reaping for learning to be planets instead of moons!

PART II

Obstacles to the Journey

4

Updating Your Defenses

I n part one, we have taken a close look at the direction of our
spiritual trek toward life. We have focused on the greatest
commandment, being teachable and honoring the uniqueness of
our personal journey. During this second section of our study,
we will highlight the fact that because we have an enemy, our
pilgrimage may sometimes seem more like an obstacle course.
The presence of evil in our world means nothing will be without
complication. Often our movement toward God's design for our
lives is met with resistance and traps that are designed to frustrate, discourage, or destroy us.

The first category of obstacles we will examine falls into the
realm of coping devices or defense mechanisms. This field of study
is so important because in many ways our defenses define our psychological health. The way we defend ourselves from the anxiety
of this world tends to fall along a continuum from unhealthy to
healthy. For example, most of us have known someone during our
life who has battled some sort of addiction. Chemical dependency
has led to untold misery for many. It is a powerful trap because it
usually begins as a way to cope with emotional pain, and it may
work to bring temporary relief. However, if one continues to drink
from that same well over and over to escape pain rather than

facing it and truly solving problems, the defense that we erected to protect a vulnerable part of us can over time become a thick prison wall or stronghold that places us in bondage. Another primitive defense that can come into play for the addict is a sense of denial. Even though people around them can see the negative impact of the addictive pattern, the person in bondage can be blinded to the path of disaster that is right in front of them.

One of my favorite ways to teach people about defense mechanisms is to look at the animal kingdom. God has equipped creatures with all kinds of clever ways to survive a hostile environment, and often these defenses illustrate something we also do as human beings. For example, in our discussion about denial, have you ever heard the phrase, "sticking your head in the sand?" That phrase comes from a myth about ostriches. It was once believed that under threatening conditions, the ostrich would literally stick its head in the sand and hope the threat would just pass by. It would be like receiving an overdue notice on our electric or water service and choosing to throw the bill in the trash. It is not there on the counter anymore to remind us of our dilemma, but the threat has not really disappeared. The consequences are still looming.

For the record, ostriches do put their heads in the sand, but only to check on their eggs. They have been known to lay down on the sand if they feel they can hide or camouflage that way. Ostriches can outrun nearly anything, and they have the kick of a mule—much better defenses! If they truly relied upon denial as their coping strategy, they would likely be extinct by now.

Turtles model for us "going into a shell." The octopus uses an inky "smokescreen." If you get too close to a duck's nest, it will act like it is wounded as a "diversionary tactic." Skunks can spray you with something you never ever want to smell like. Have you ever gotten too close to someone's issues, and they let you have it with all kinds of stinky words or behaviors? You get the idea. Animals and people have many defense systems at their disposal. Defense is sometimes needed in this threatening world, but as we will see, the way that we defend is an important skill to learn through the obstacle course of life. For a more extensive list of common defense mechanisms, one can simply type that phrase into a web search and find many helpful lists and charts. Can you think of a way that you have coped with life in the past that has come back to bite you later?

How Defenses Form

One of the reasons counselors like to look at a person's early family life is the information this provides into the formation of a person's defense system. People who grow up in a relatively healthy family naturally gain experience in managing the ups and downs of life. This often includes a growing ability to trust and a sense that attachments are secure. Every kid faces their share of hard knocks along the way and no parent is perfect, but if the home base is providing adequate love, emotional attunement, and good coaching, most youngsters typically learn to handle life's emotional challenges and do not need to lean so heavily on high powered defenses to survive emotionally.

It is not within the scope of this book to cover this in depth, but there are certainly indicators that genetic components also impact the defenses one might latch onto. Good parenting does not guarantee healthier defense systems, but it clearly increases the odds.

However, when you think about family struggles such as abandonment, neglect, abuse, or trauma, the formation of defenses can take on a whole other dimension. Consider the following examples of emotionally charged family dynamics:

- One child is clearly favored over another in the home.

- You can often hear your parents yelling at each other when you are trying to go to sleep.

- You are four years old, and a family member is regularly molesting you.

- No matter how hard you try, you mostly get criticism from one of your parents.

- Your house is often so dirty it is embarrassing to invite your friends over.

What are your hunches about how a child might adapt to these kinds of situations? When we are young, the shaping of our coping skills typically develops by trial and error. Most people kind of stumble onto something that helps them feel better in an anxiety-provoking situation. If that thought or behavior helps us be calmer in a pinch, we are likely to turn to it again and again. For example, abuse victims can sometimes report that they have found a way to dissociate during the inescapable horror they are experiencing. It is as if the mind finds a way to say, "I am not strong enough to keep this abuse from happening to me, but I will check out in my mind and not be present."

That dissociative ability that can help a person survive nightmarish moments can also lead to a fracture at the deeper levels of the mind and soul. All of us have those times where we feel a bit divided inside, but for those who are battling those unhealed fractures, it can literally feel like a Dr. Jekyll/Mr. Hyde kind of life where one is often surprised by what comes out during those high anxiety moments.

Some of the most puzzling behaviors of people can be explained by looking at them as defenses gone wrong. A person who has fallen into a self-harm behavior such as scratching or cutting themselves will often explain that the pain inflicted on their bodies is somehow better than the level of emotional pain they are experiencing on the inside. Someone with an eating disorder might tell you that it is driven by an oppressive, perfectionistic internal standard that they just cannot seem to escape.

Please understand, not all defenses are bad, and even the more primitive defenses have at times helped people survive horrendous life experiences. But if our goal is to enter and thrive on the Christian journey, we will have to examine the armor we are wearing and evaluate whether we can clink around in it all the way to the promised land. As you take a close look at your life, past and present, what would you say are the primary coping skills you have leaned on to get through life at this point?

A Biblical Look at Defenses

Hebrew 12:1–2 states, "Therefore, since we are surrounded by such a great cloud of witnesses, let us throw off everything that hinders and the sin that so easily entangles. And let us run with perseverance the race marked out for us, fixing our eyes on Jesus, the pioneer and perfecter of faith."

This race that the Hebrew writer says we are to run by faith sounds very much like the journey I am trying to describe. He has provided his own case studies in the previous chapter (Heb 11) and now builds on that to spur us on toward our journey. The phrase I want to target for this chapter of our study is "sin that so easily entangles." From my research, these words could literally be translated "sin that skillfully surrounds us." This feels like another of those key areas where a psychological concept and a Biblical truth intersect.

Defenses form as a repeated behavior that begins as the construction of a wall or a force field to protect us. But, as the layers of protection accumulate over time, the chosen behaviors and attitudes of defense surround and enclose us like a prison wall. As mentioned earlier, a stronghold or fortress now oppresses us into a habit or pattern that we struggle to set aside or do without. Our freedom is greatly restricted. This generally drives us away from a life of faith and trust in God, and toward a man-made armor that relies on our own strategizing to ward off anxiety.

Our outdated defenses can be obvious things like chemical dependency, deception, or rage. They can also be more subtle such as blame-shifting, legalism, or passive-aggressive behavior. Regardless of our coping choices, a life of faith is the antidote for our defensive strongholds. If we are to run unhindered, we face the challenge Jesus has given us to define our life by faith in him.

It is interesting that the Bible includes an entire section to describe the "armor of God." The social sciences teach us that our anxiety is set in motion as a response to a threat. Ephesians 6:10–18 makes it clear that the ultimate threat is our struggle against the very real evil that exists in this world. God has designed and ordained a defense system that includes elements such as truth, righteousness, the gospel of peace, faith, and salvation.

The bottom line of the apostle Paul's illustration of the armor is this. As it sinks in that God is for you and loves you, that your eternal future is secured, and that God will strengthen you over time to face truth and live a life that is more in sync with your conscience, then you will develop a new set of tools to face life's anxieties. Psychology indicates that when anxiety is triggered, we will fight, take flight, or freeze. In Eph 6, the key words are none of these, but rather "stand" and "pray."

Building on this spiritual element of God's armor, my personal favorite "go-to" verses regarding anxiety are found in Phil 4:6–7. The Spirit encourages us to pray when we are anxious. I do not get the sense that this mandate to pray magically makes our anxiety go away, but a life of learning to trust God with our fears and turning to him does lead to a "peace that surpasses all understanding." This peace is said to "guard our hearts and minds in Christ Jesus." The word "guard" in this passage is a military term which is all about a defense system. It literally means to place a series of guards around our hearts and minds. The heart is the emotional center and the mind is the cognitive center of a person—our most vital and vulnerable organs.

The most high-tech coping strategy we possess is our growing trust in a reliable God; however, learning to trust is no small undertaking, correct? How has your walk with God helped you cope with anxiety? Regardless of your faith, what things do you find still take you down the path of being an anxious person?

I have been speaking of anxiety from an emotional and spiritual perspective, but it is also important to clarify that anxiety can be a medical issue. I have counseled with my share of people who feel incredibly guilty because their faith is not enough to overcome the anxiousness that plagues them. While growing in our faith can certainly help us in our anxiety battle, things like panic attacks, obsessive-compulsive behaviors, and phobias can most certainly have a body chemistry component. Seeing a doctor and exploring medication may be crucial in helping you be at your best and strongest as you fight this important battle against anxiety.

Defensive Restructuring

When David was preparing to fight Goliath, King Saul dressed David in a suit of armor that did not work for him (1 Sam 17:38–39). David felt more comfortable with a sling and five stones. His defense included these simple things, but his real defense was his trust in God and his life experience fighting off a lion or a bear if they tried to attack his sheep. However, not all of us have the faith or courage of David. Most of us find that trading our old man-made armor is a very uncomfortable experience.

With my clients, I often refer to this period of defensive restructuring as a time of "emotional homelessness." We have come to know that our old way of coping is no longer effective, but often our new strategies are not yet perfected. It can feel like leaving a dilapidated building but the new construction is not yet completed. What is one to do? In the Old Testament story of the exodus, it was hard for the people when they were in between Egypt and the promised land. Their old way of life was bondage and slavery, but it would take a while to get to their new home. Their emotional homelessness grew so uncomfortable that many of them wanted to go back to their old world of slavery. It is not unusual to see the same temptation in today's world.

While in the wilderness, they dwelled in tents. It will feel this way for those who are trading outdated defenses for the armor of God. I suspect it may be something like what happens when a snake sheds its skin. It must feel like a time of great vulnerability, and yet it is a necessary step if the animal is to grow. I feel a deep empathy for people who find themselves in these hard transitions. I am sure God is keenly attuned to our cries when we find ourselves in the desert seasons of our trek.

So, the question becomes "how do we update or restructure our defenses?" As is the case in many areas, change often begins with a growing self-awareness. If you have taken the time to slow down and study your behaviors, and you can now identify your primary coping devices, then you have taken an important first step.

The next phase falls into a category I like to call counting the cost. Sometimes, once we know what we are paying to manage life the way we do, it gets our attention and provides more motivation to make changes. For example, if smoking cigarettes is a choice you have made to feel calmer, keep your weight down, or feel more accepted by your peers, how would you calculate those costs? There are visible things like the dollar amount per pack and the discoloration of your skin, but what are the hidden price tags?

Let's say you have chosen avoidance as your defense. What impact may it have on a married person if you change the subject every time your spouse wants to have an in-depth conversation? How many opportunities for advancement in your career have been lost because you have learned to avoid new things that might be hard?

How would you assess the financial, emotional, relational, and spiritual cost-benefit of hoarding, shopping, gambling, praying, time on electronics, sleeping, hobbies, reading, exercise, stuffing feelings down, isolation, controlling, playing the victim, attention seeking, self-centeredness, and codependency? As you can see, there are many questions to be asked and many assessments to be made, so do your best to be clear about what your coping behaviors are costing or contributing to your life. Our entanglements can greatly slow us down on our journey, or at worst, some of them can be like quicksand and take us under. What cost are you tired of paying regarding your defense system?

The third element of updating our armor becomes "practice" or "discipline." This is where our grace toward ourselves is particularly important. It is not so hard to start the change process but finishing it can be demanding. There are few shortcuts to our armor updates. This is one of the areas where I am so grateful for the godly upbringing that I received. The Christian faith is loaded with spiritual practices that teach you how to say "no" to the self. Concepts like prayer, fasting, Bible study, service, and solitude are all disciplines that build spiritual muscle and help you be ready when life's pressure is coming at you. As we know from our time in the gym, muscle building is not an instant process. No pain, no gain. Whether it is dribbling a basketball, playing a musical instrument, mastering chess, or becoming a more mature person, it is typically a process. Training is more important than trying harder. Being patient with oneself is more valuable than being critical or giving up.

I have always been intrigued by someone who has had a breakthrough with a tough habit they have been working to overcome. They may be on the fourteenth attempt to create a healthier way to cope. Why did the breakthrough not come on the first thirteen efforts? Research seems to indicate that there are all kinds of little micro changes going on between our attempts, and these efforts sometimes cascade into a major readiness to complete the armor update. This is one more reason to place ourselves in positions to train and practice. To keep on asking, seeking, and knocking (Matt 7:7) with God's help increases the likelihood that we will break a stronghold. So, be self-aware. Do the audit of your defenses and practice, practice, practice. God will not waste any of your suffering if allowed to be your personal trainer.

Case Study—Jase

I think all counselors would relate to that experience when every now and then a new client steps into your office for the first time and there is an immediate sense of connection. You just somehow know that this journey is going to be special. That was my sense with Jase. My early impression of him was captured by the word "gifted."

Jase is bright and articulate. The insights that he grasped, without much prompting on my part, were notable. He was in his early thirties but had already accomplished some significant things in his career. He has a very engaging personality and would rival some of Hollywood's best for his good looks.

Jase has been married for six years to a delightful young woman who teaches elementary school, and they have a vivacious three-year-old that they both love very much. Jase's presenting problems were a nagging low-grade depression and a desire to break free from his use of pornography. His wife was very supportive of Jase in this battle, but also felt brokenhearted by having to deal with this rival in her marriage.

As Jase unfolded his story it helped us begin to piece together the factors that contributed to the development of his defenses. He described his dad in very frustrating terms. Jase observed that no matter what he tried to speak to his dad about, it became about his dad. These narcissistic traits showed up in his parent's marriage and led to its demise. His mom seemed emotionally lost in some codependent quicksand after the divorce, which meant some other unhealthy men in and out of Jase's life. He knew his mom loved him, but there was little steadiness to their family structure. There was no Christian influence, and Jase remembered being in a situation where he was pretty much on his own regarding how he began to build his life.

I have a great deal of empathy for teenage guys and gals who are highly attractive people. It can be both a blessing and a curse. It is not difficult gaining a bunch of attention, but it creates all kinds of potential pitfalls in the realm of sexual exploration and opportunities. This was especially true for Jase since there was not much supervision of his life during adolescence. Unsurprisingly, he developed that "be-with-as-many-girls-as-you-can" philosophy, which provided a powerful defense system against the boredom and emotional aloneness that often haunted him. In the throes of all that, while still in his college years, Jase met a woman fifteen years older than him whom he lived with for a few months. She seemed bent on making all their fantasies come true.

During this season of his life, Jase never really experienced much grief or sadness regarding his exploits. It simply was not in his ethic to feel bad about being with all these women. But he then met a friend in college whose family was a healthy example of authentic faith. They brought him into their circle and modeled some things that he had never experienced. Over time, Jase began to understand the gospel and wanted to be a disciple of Jesus. He also met Sara in college and later married her. He has worked hard to be faithful to her. But, as you might guess, the old defenses were still a stronghold. While pornography was the battle, Jase indicated the more basic fight was an internal one. Even if he did not access a website that crossed his new boundaries, there were so many images and memories embedded in his mind that he really did not need to go any further than his thought process to reenter the old forms of coping with boredom and aloneness.

Jase was deeply grateful to have a safe setting in therapy to be honest about his internal world, and to be met with the balance of grace and truth he wanted even as a child. Because of the giftedness I mentioned earlier, he made great progress in therapy. He read everything I suggested and his pace of forward movement was quite amazing. This progression took many forms. Jase found out his dad was in therapy, and though he lived in a different state, Jase made some efforts to reconnect. Though his dad still had some remnants of his self-absorbed style, they were able to talk about Jase's painful memories of his dad not being there in the early years. This reconnection allowed Jase to turn loose of some the anger he had harbored toward his father.

Jase began to have a greater understanding of his own identity (as we discussed in chapter 3). He recognized that by nature he is a risk-taker, an entrepreneur, and needs some emotional and spiritual elbow room to be who God created him to be. He wanted to be free of lustful thoughts, but he could not see himself as the kind of guy who would settle into a nine-to-five job and sit on the couch at night when he came home. He is active, social, and even in his spiritual life, he is drawn to "out of the box" ideas about how to impact God's kingdom. It was a joy to watch Jase discover these things about himself and to realize that they were good and not somehow defective.

It also made sense to invite Sara in for a few sessions, which she was glad to do. Even though she and her family are more conservative in their approach to life, because of the progress Jase was making in redesigning his defenses, she was able to bless his adventuresome side. She understood that some men have an extra measure of wildness to them, and if harnessed and within the boundaries of God's will, that can be a wonderful thing.

Some months after Jase terminated therapy, I spoke with him and he reminded me of another very important insight about the impact of our defenses. He said, "The defenses I built allowed me to completely avoid confronting any emotion. I am realizing this more and more lately as I find myself feeling emotional over things that historically did nothing to me. Things like TV shows with emotional endings, and more prevalent, moments with my son that bring tears to my eyes. My defenses gave me a false sense of control and progress in life, all the while I was missing out on what could really be."

Defenses can dull our emotions to the pain, but at the same time, they tend to blunt our ability to experience life-giving emotions. This is another significant price we pay for outdated coping strategies. It has been so good to see Jase flourishing in his business and deeply enjoying his role as a husband and father. He took up golf as a new part of his coping skill set, and as you might anticipate, quickly became very good at it. I feel certain that Jase will always have to keep an eye on the desires of the flesh, but he has found a more fitting suit of armor and I pray it serves him well all his days.

Can you identify any ways that your journey relates to Jase's? How is God harnessing your strength, giftedness, or even your wildness to accomplish some of the things he is calling you to do?

5

Regulating Emotions

I want to begin this chapter with a few reflective questions. In general, do you believe that having emotions and feelings is a good thing or a bad thing? Chances are you said something like "it depends." If so, what does it depend on? What do you think the world would be like if human beings had no emotion?

Most of us have no problem with positive emotions such as feeling joyful or peaceful. However, when we experience feelings such as fear, boredom, or anger, that can be another story. To avoid the destruction that can be caused by mishandling negative emotions, it is essential to learn to regulate them. If we do not develop this skill, we are likely to experience more than our share of misery and leave a trail of relational damage behind us.

The Purpose of Negative Emotions

Several years ago, I remember sitting in an anger regulation workshop led by Dr. Steven Stosny. He has done some fascinating research on several topics that I encourage you to explore, but the thing that stood out to me most that day was his statement that negative emotions have purpose.[1] They do not appear just to annoy us, but they have meaning that can be very helpful to us. Our emotions are not the enemy.

At one time or another, I think most of us have asked God why we must endure the unpleasantness of feelings such as sadness, frustration, or panic. From all the research that has been done about negative emotions, the best guess we have about their purpose is that they point us to a problem that needs to be solved. Our feelings can be signaling devices that something is not right. Just as pain is an indicator that something is not right in our bodies, painful emotions are designed to grab our attention that something is amiss in our life in general.

No one likes to feel pain, but have you ever thought about what might happen if it did not exist? If I cut myself while chopping vegetables, pain motivates me to not only bandage the wound, but be more careful next time. It is my understanding that leprosy patients lose their fingers and toes over time because the disease leads to a loss of nerve endings in the extremities. No pain, no attention to damage, thus the loss.

Anxiety gives us a clue that we are feeling threatened in some way. Anger alerts us to some sort of emotional wound that has occurred. Grief is a normal reaction to something being lost. If we view the emotion as a flashing red light to get our attention, we have a much better chance of using our resources to find solutions. This helps us feel empowered, whereas if we are simply upset about feeling bad, we typically end up feeling like a powerless victim.

Negative emotions did not exist in the garden of Eden before sin entered the world, and in the future when God makes everything new, there will be no threats, so negative emotions will again be unnecessary. But in the meantime, it is our task to understand them and navigate them, lest they become the obstacle that blocks us and reduces the effectiveness of our current journey.

---

1. Workshop led by Dr. Steven Stosny at Gaithersburg, MD. I have integrated Dr. Stosny's concepts into my teaching for years and I am sure his influence is visible in this chapter.

The Bible approaches emotions in a very matter of fact way. Statements like "fear not" or "cast your anxiety on God" give us a clue that our emotions are normal and everyone experiences them. The emphasis is on emotional management. For example, when the apostle Paul says, "In your anger do not sin. Do not let the sun go down while you are still angry" (Eph 4:26), he makes it clear that being angry is not sinful, but there also seems to be a clear warning that it can become destructive if we do not harness it properly.

My favorite illustration for anger is fire. We know the horrendous damage that is done by fire when it is out of control. It is heart-breaking to watch the news and see the destructive nature of a forest fire or see someone's house going up in flames. If you have ever visited a burn unit in the hospital, you know the devastating power of fire when it is out of control. But fire in and of itself is not a bad thing. Fire can be used to heat our homes, cook our meals, or power our cars. However, in those cases, it is contained and controlled. Anger, when corralled properly, is the same way. How many positive changes and reforms have begun because someone was angry about an injustice? For instance, the organization Mothers Against Drunk Driving (MADD) is a group of people who are appropriately angry about the loss of a loved one in a drunk-driving crash. They harnessed their anger to care for those who are grieving and to change the laws about driving while impaired.

The Old Testament prophets were at times incensed about the behavior of God's people who were supposed to accurately represent the Lord to the nations. They spoke truth in a bold way to bring Israel back to its senses. Jesus himself displayed anger on occasion at the hypocrisy of the religious leaders of his day. The emotion is not bad, but it is like a power tool and requires control and caution to use it in a constructive way.

The Crucial Skill of Self-Control

In the world of emotions, there are numerous ways to mismanage them. Some people are led by their emotions, though emotions are not good leaders. Some try to escape emotions by alcohol or drug use. Others press emotions down and try to pretend they do not exist or are not important, thus setting themselves up for a volcanic eruption or an ulcer. However, biblical wisdom tells us that the real goal is a quality called "self-control."

Self-control is a fruit of the Spirit (Gal 5:22–23), and the most basic meaning of that term is "a mastery of the self." This means we get the self to behave in the way we intend. The bottom line of this concept is that the self must be disciplined if it is to have the capacity to guide us in the way we genuinely want to go.

I realize this is not an easy idea to grasp. Perhaps it becomes simpler if we go at it from another angle. Wrestle with this question. If I am not in control of me, what are the other options? Would you agree that one can be controlled by another person, an addictive substance, or the demonic?

There are also more subtle battles on the inside of us for self-control. What happens when people are out of control with their spending, their weight, or their temper? In addition to outside forces vying for control, internally we are not altogether integrated into a single voice. Sometimes we are conflicted and there is a battle for who gets the final decisive word. In the psychology world, this process is sometimes referred to as "executive functioning."

Executive function is a business metaphor that describes a set of thinking processes and mental skills that help us plan and successfully execute our goals. Just as a business has a chief executive that monitors all the different departments so that the company can move forward effectively, so the human mind has many sources of input. You have probably heard someone talk about having a committee in their head. Our executive function listens to all the input and then makes decisions that hopefully represent the self well.

We hear numerous lessons, as we should, on our relationship with God and our relationship with others. But I have heard fewer sermons on how to relate to the self. The Bible is not silent on this subject. Jesus commanded us to love others as ourselves (Matt 22:39), which seems to indicate that our self-care should be a good measuring tool for the way we care for others. We are also encouraged to

- examine the self (1 Cor 11:28; 2 Cor 13:5),
- deny the self (Matt 16:24),
- not be self-willed (Titus 1:7; 2 Pet 2:10),
- control the self (Titus 2:12).

It becomes clearer when we study these passages in depth that the best self is a disciplined self. This makes sense as we recognize that the self is not a good master in our flawed condition. If the self has what it wants, it will likely become a cruel taskmaster; but taught and disciplined by God's Spirit, human beings can display amazing qualities that put the self in its proper place.

So, the key question for us at this juncture is "how do you feel about your self-control, especially in the realm of negative emotions like anger, fear, and sadness?"

Are you making these emotions work for you to solve problems, or do these feelings chronically take you somewhere you do not want to go and lead to unwanted results, making you feel like a victim?

If the goal of regulating emotion is reached by more effective control of the self, where do we begin? How do I gain skill in this vital area? Like many things in our spiritual journey, the answer is two-fold. There are clues when we take a close look at our past, and there are important things to examine in the here and now. Let us look at both.

The Development of Frustration Tolerance

I suspect that all of us would agree that the world can be a very frustrating place. There are simple things like always seeming to pick the slowest check-out line, unwanted soliciting phone calls, or sitting right in front of a very annoying person at a big event. But there are also deep and painful frustrations such as a very costly repair when your bank account is at its lowest, someone you thought was a friend stabbing you in the back, or discovering you are now facing a chronic illness that will greatly limit your life.

What sorts of things frustrate you the most these days? Our ability to navigate these emotion-laden moments is greatly affected by the skill level we have developed to tolerate frustration. Like many character traits that we need to develop, this one is often linked to the kind of training ground we had in our growing-up years. As infants, we all start with the same inability to deal with frustration. When we got hungry, wet, or uncomfortable in any other way, we did not think to ourselves, "Oh, Mommy and Daddy might be sleeping so I will wait a little longer before I cry." No, we did what we were designed to do: we cried to get the required attention and let the world know we were frustrated.

As we got a little older, say the terrible twos, we learned the art of the tantrum to get someone to alleviate our frustration. But what if a person never learns a better way to manage the negative emotion being felt? Do you see any evidence in our world that people can be in a twenty-, thirty-, or forty-year-old body, yet still be throwing a two-year-old temper tantrum? It can be a scary thing to realize that some people have never learned the art of managing tantrums but are now able to carry a weapon and unleash their frustration on an unsuspecting school, workplace, or community.

So how do we teach frustration tolerance, so that people are more able to manage the powerful emotions that come at them? Some of the research here is very interesting. Children seem to do very well at learning how to tolerate frustration if it is given in very small doses over long periods of time with a healthy amount of patience and love along the way. We all know that frustration is hard to swallow at any age, but if we face it bit by bit, so that we can properly digest or metabolize it, we find ourselves more able over time to accept the things we cannot change. We get better at "living life on life's terms," one of the most powerful phrases from the world of Alcoholics Anonymous and twelve-step programs.

So, the crucial parenting advice here is to avoid two destructive extremes. Frustration tolerance does not get constructed well if we frustrate our children in too large a dose or if we do not allow our children to be frustrated enough. In the first of these two scenarios, we are talking about things like neglect and abuse. If a child faces these intolerable levels of frustration without consistent love and reassurance, the heart of a youngster is overwhelmed and there is no ability to absorb the potential lessons about the hard parts of life. It is like a flooding rain that destroys and runs off the land rather than soaking in a way that is helpful.

In the second extreme, a parent is so determined to protect the child from disappointment or anything painful that the home tends to become child-centered, which can lead to very little practice at being frustrated and learning how to self-soothe. Imagine the disappointment of facing the real world in adulthood and finding that the world really does not revolve around you. This, too, is a recipe for being frustrated yet not knowing how to manage the accompanying emotional storm.

As a growing number of families struggle to provide a healthy emotional environment, we see an alarming trend on the evening news where more and more people with less self-control are acting out their frustration in deeply destructive ways. While some people turn their anger on others, just as many internalize their deep frustration. This can lead to esteem-damaging messages, self-harm, and even suicide.

It is important that we find effective ways of fighting back against this tide and recognize how we can overcome the challenging obstacle of managing emotion. There is a great deal of research being done in this field, so if you want to study this concept further, just type "emotional dysregulation" into your Google search and be prepared for the seemingly endless amount of information that is being generated in that part of the psychological world.

The Bible is packed with helpful concepts regarding frustration tolerance and self-control. Any consistent and genuine effort that one makes at Christian discipleship is bound to be helpful at better managing negative emotions. I love the fact that Scripture makes it clear this world will be a very frustrating place and we should not be surprised by this reality. First Peter 4:12 is an impacting verse that reminds us of this truth. "Dear friends, do not be surprised at the fiery ordeal that has come on you to test you, as though something strange were happening to you." As we have discussed previously, this world is badly broken, and frustration abounds. But as one realizes this and creates a different framework for responding to the suffering, Paul indicates that we can learn the secret of contentment regardless of life's circumstances (Phil 4:11–12).

For those who did not naturally gain frustration-tolerance skills in their youth, it is very important to begin to focus on regular ways to practice this needed skill. Your Christian walk should assist you in a general way, but targeting specific ways to practice will accelerate the development of your emotional muscle in this area. Before we move to the next section, take a moment to give yourself a school letter grade for your current level of frustration tolerance.

Regulation in the Here and Now

Years ago, one of my pastoral counseling supervisors, Dr. James Hyde, taught me that feelings are like a flood, and our thought processes about those feelings are like our pipes and valves and locks and dams that assist us in our flood control efforts. Thus, there is real value when the flood comes that we are ready to begin "thinking" about the needed solutions that our negative emotions may be alerting us to.

For example, think about the emotions you see out there driving in traffic. We are forced to share the road with people who have all kinds of different driving habits and styles. Which of the following is most likely to spark some emotion (anxiety, anger, indignation, disgust, etc.) in you?

- Someone right up on your bumper
- Someone barely going the speed limit in the fast lane
- Someone holding their cell phone and talking while driving

- Someone weaving in and out of traffic at a high
  rate of speed

- Someone waiting until the last minute to get in
  the correct lane to exit

- Someone honking their horn or giving an obscene gesture
  in your direction

Because driving in today's world can be so emotionally provoking, I find it a good place to practice my emotional regulation. I am most triggered by aggressive drivers, so when I see someone endangering others by their driving style, and I am tempted to pull out my invisible bazooka and blast them off the road (no aggression there, right?), I try to move toward some helpful thoughts that allow me to exhibit a calmer response. These thoughts include the following:

- I wonder why that person is in such a hurry.
  I am glad I am not.

- It seems like that guy (or gal) never learned much
  about being a team player, how sad.

- My goal is to get safely from A to B, do not let my
  competitive side get hooked here.

This principle of using thoughts to manage emotions has been around for a long time, but now we have even more scientific evidence as to why it can be helpful. Now that we have equipment that can see brain activity more clearly, we have learned some intriguing things about what is really going on in this marvelous control center inside our skull. When we are calm, brain activity is strongest in the part of the brain that is known for our best wisdom. However, when we are emotionally charged, brain activity slows down in that part of the brain and picks up in the part of the brain that is known more for defense and survival skills.

This is one reason why emotions are not good leaders. They are excellent signaling devices, but negative emotions often put us on guard and our best common sense loses its voice. This defensive part of the brain can often be impulsive and have no filters. Can you think of a time when you reacted to a situation that surprised you and left you feeling like "where did that response come from?" I liken this to the response you can get if you corner a typically docile animal. It will often come out fighting. When defenses activate, it can end up feeling like a "not me" kind of experience.

People that become proficient at regulating emotion are those who become avid students of this process. I encourage people to "autopsy" their anger events. Go back and dissect everything you can to understand what triggered you, what your thought process was, and what you would like to do differently next time this sort of thing occurs. This helps us not waste our suffering and instead broaden the de-escalation skills that are so important to our success in navigating our emotional world.

Some of you by nature have a longer fuse than others when it comes to emotional management. But if you are one of those people who has a short fuse, I think you will find it gratifying to dig in and learn more about self-control in this area. Back in the day, we were on the right track when we were encouraged to "count to ten" to stay calm when we were emotionally charged. Now we know so much more as to why that is important. If you can keep your body calm, your brain has a much better chance of utilizing wisdom rather than becoming survival oriented and taking no prisoners.

People sometimes ask me why there is so much emphasis on things like breathing exercises. Breathing in rhythmic ways forces one to focus and think. For some, this facilitates giving the brain something to focus on and keeps the emotional flood at bay until we access greater control. Buying ourselves a bit of time in emotionally provoking situations aids self-control. Emotions such as anger can be like electricity. They are very fast and take the path of least resistance, so it is even more important to have a few extra seconds to think clearly and make our best decisions.

As we consider terms such as mindfulness, self-awareness, and executive function, I cannot help but think about the very important biblical concept of a renewed mind (Rom 12:2). As we learn to pay more attention to our thought process and invite God to transform it, we will be in a much better place to make emotions work for us instead of against us.

So, in summary, emotions are a gift and they are very much a part of what makes us human. Negative emotions have purpose and exist to signal us that there is a problem to solve. Emotions are not good leaders, and to gain healthy control over them, we must exercise our thought process to craft wise solutions to the problems our emotions point us toward.

The Spirit of God is with us to help us master the self in ways that discipline our life and allow us to maximize our executive function so that we keep step with the mission God has called us to. Take a few minutes to record your most significant insights from this chapter.

Case Study—Mick and Allison

In the initial stages of marriage counseling, I remember Mick and Allison agreeing that when their relationship was good, it was really good, but when it was bad, it was really bad. They are both quite personable and easy to like, so it intrigued me as to how things could get so volatile.

Both Mick and Allison have had their share of trauma in life. Mick's dad was a mean-spirited, abusive character. His mom was described as incredibly manipulative and deceitful. Positive memories of childhood are rare for Mick. He also felt a heavy responsibility to protect his younger brother from verbal and physical abuse that could break out without much warning.

When Allison was a youngster, her father crossed sexual boundaries with her, which destroyed trust and laid the groundwork for much confusion and shame. Allison deeply loved her mom, but she died from cancer when Allison was ten years old. It was no surprise that Allison struggled through adolescence and developed some very unhealthy coping strategies.

It became very clear in the early stages of marital therapy that Mick and Allison could do very well during low stress times in their lives. But as soon as things became emotionally charged, and either of them began working out of their old survival skills, the tension and conflict were on. Over time, in our safe environment, Mick was able to admit that he could become like his father and be verbally abusive, threatening, and intimidating toward Allison.

Allison has a strong personality of her own, so she is no push-over. She has read and studied a great deal over the course of her life and could outdebate Mick on nearly any subject in the world of self-help. Allison would acknowledge she has had to work on her control issues and that she can over-function trying to please Mick when perhaps he just needs some space from her.

There are many moving parts to the complex journey I have had with Mick and Allison, but for the sake of this chapter, I want to look primarily at the importance of regulating emotion and how that has impacted their marriage. For Mick, he has worked very hard on managing anger while Allison's key growth has come in the form of regulating anxiety and fear.

We have talked earlier in the chapter about brain function during calm times and emotionally-charged moments. Mick's "at-ease" brain and his "triggered" brain could not be more different. This is a guy who is very bright. He runs a business and is great with his customers. He loves missions and has been very involved with helping the poor and disenfranchised. He can tend to give away too much of his time and skill, and as a result has been taken advantage of because of his kindness. On good days, he would do anything to make his wife happy, and he still provides care for his aging father who to this day is still stuck in his meanness.

However, when he is working out of the reptilian part of his brain (those primitive survival skills), he can cuss like a sailor, get a very different look in his eye, threaten divorce, and become a very intimidating force. On more than one occasion, after getting into a conflict with Allison while at a restaurant, he angrily refused to get in the car with her and walked ten miles home in the dark just to prove a point. Then he would be deeply apologetic the next day for putting her through that.

Allison has been very torn about how to deal with Mick's Dr. Jekyll/Mr. Hyde moments. There have been times where she has felt the need to get away from his verbal abuse. She did separate for a time, but ultimately decided to return to the marriage and they have been working hard to understand and manage what they now call their "are-you-kidding-me?" moments.

As you might imagine, Allison can be hyperalert to what is going on in the relationship. Her anxiety about the next potential argument can cause her to try to cover every contingency in an effort to keep bad things from happening. In marital conversations, she would often feel like she was defending herself and getting into lengthy explanations as to why she said what she said. This, too, would be maddening for Mick, and could work as a trigger to his frustration.

The therapeutic journey has been slow and painful at times. Mick has a love-hate relationship with counseling. I mean, think about it: what guy would want to spend numerous sessions taking a recent marital-conflict event, slowing it down, dissecting it, studying it, and discussing what might be better next time? There is so much potential for shame and rekindled emotion. Who wouldn't be tempted to just avoid, blame, and defend—especially if that has been your default setting all your life?

But the surprising grace and friendship Mick has felt in therapy keep him willing to peel back the layers and be more honest and vulnerable. We now laugh together when he says, "I'm done with therapy!" because he always comes back and often talks about the ways it is helping, even though it is painful. Part of him still expects the punitive reaction he always received from his father, but there is a deepening recognition that he is loved, even though he is a work in progress. Mick would tell you that his ability to use his thinking faculties more effectively has reduced his volatile anger events by 80 percent, and we are still progressing.

Allison loves therapy. She is a processor by nature, and loves to read and apply spiritual and psychological insights. I know it is hard for Mick sometimes because he probably feels like there are two counselors in the room ganging up on him. However, Mick and Allison are truly realizing who the real enemy is, and it is certainly not their spouse. They have both had many opportunities to leave and call it quits, but they have chosen not to do that. Evil would love to exploit their past traumas and have them lead with their fiery emotions, but their growing reservoir of wisdom now tells them that blaming is of little value and it is time to stay focused on the one thing they can control—their selves. All three of us regularly celebrate the progress, reiterate the goal, and work toward effective solutions as a team.

Recently, I knew we had reached a new level of trust and forward movement when Mick invited Allison into his business to "work her magic" with the organizational and administrative piece of the company. These are her strengths and his weaknesses, and they had talked about her helping him out in these areas for years. But previous attempts always ended up mirroring the tension in the marriage. Allison would jump in with her strength of personality to make changes. This would feel like control to Mick, and he would become frustrated and take things back over himself, even though he did not like the administrative part of the business. Mick is great at sales and service, but details and paperwork would fall behind, his stress would increase, and it would spill over into their home life.

Now that they can talk more and see each other's perspective more graciously, they are getting to that place where each of them can do what they do best and feel like a team. Regulating emotion and using one's best wisdom goes a long way in establishing peace. I suspect this skill building process will need to go on for a long time in Mick and Allison's world, but they are both committed to self-control, and the Spirit of God is glad to be invited into that realm of their lives.

6

Travel Companions

I n our discussion of obstacles on our spiritual journey, we have looked at whether our defenses are helping or dragging us down and we have examined whether our emotions are working for or against us. The third potential obstacle to be aware of involves the people around us and in our heads.

I suspect we all have a memory or two of being stuck in a car, on a bus, or in a room with a highly annoying person. Over time, most of us have become pretty picky about who we travel with. There is a good reason for that. Journeying is just more enjoyable if you feel at ease with the people around you.

This becomes quite the balancing act when you consider that the Bible instructs us to find fellowship with like-minded people, but also to engage the lost, the annoying, and the messy human condition all around us. As challenging as this is, thankfully we have the clear example of Jesus to help us in the construction of our boundaries so that we can both enjoy the journey and further Christ's kingdom along the way. It is interesting to study the rhythm of Jesus's life. He clearly spent a great deal of time with his disciples. Even though they were dull and frustrating at times, they were willing followers and I sense that their fellowship was rich and fulfilling for all, including Jesus.

One of my favorite verses in the Gospels is Luke 22:15. This verse informs us that Jesus "eagerly desired" to share the Passover meal with his disciples before he suffered the upcoming cross. Sometimes I feel like we get the idea that God simply tolerates us as human beings. This verse reminds us that he enjoys us and desires to be with us, despite our shortcomings.

Jesus also spent some very intentional time alone. This involved things like prayer, reflection, planning, and rest. This time alone and with his inner circle paved the way for interfacing with the crowds and his one-on-one encounters with those he was led to engage. Ideally, our times of solitude and healthy fellowship should provide a sense of sanctuary that prepares and strengthens us for the difficult work of our mission.

Time alone, time with friends, and time on mission create the kind of balance that gives our journey both meaning and sustainable power. However, there are crucial mistakes that can be made in each of these three areas. Before we tackle these one at a time, take a moment to rate each area on a scale of one to ten.

- The quality of my alone time
- The support provided by my inner circle of family/friends
- Understanding and implementing my sense of mission for God

Our Solitude

I love my time alone. There are many things that happen in that rich inner world God has given me. I ponder deep things that I do not understand. I have a vivid imagination that has no trouble envisioning things I may undertake someday. I think about things I might do for those I love. When there is conflict, I prepare for hard conversations in my mind. I talk to God and listen for the still small voice. As an introvert, being by myself is a reenergizing component of my life. It has been essential in thriving during all these years of ministry.

However, I know it is not like this for everyone. Some people struggle to be still and quickly grow restless without some sort of outside stimulus. Our culture, with all its amazing technology, does not make being still any easier. The constant notification that someone is messaging us is not easy for some to ignore. Extroverted people obviously do not need as much solitude as introverts. They are energized by being with and around people. God made them that way; however, all of us need some amount of time to think, plan, pray, and be comfortable with the quiet.

Beyond these God-given differences in personality, there are other factors that can greatly impact the quality of one's time alone. For this study, we will look at two: self-esteem (do I like who I am becoming?) and self-talk (what am I saying to myself?).

Esteem is a tricky concept for those who are committed to following a perfect God. Just being in God's presence makes us more aware of our sin. I am convinced this is one reason people are resistant to draw near to God. Without an understanding of grace, the Christian life can just make you feel worse about yourself. Like seeing all the dust particles in your home when the sun shines through, our stepping into the light of God's perfection shows more of our blemishes. As we have discussed, this explains the temptation to hide and defend. So, how do we feel at peace in our time alone if we are regularly made aware by our conscience that we fall short?

The good news of the new covenant is freedom from the law and its impact (Rom 8:1–2). Given the opportunity, God will begin to overhaul our conscience and provide us a very different way of measuring ourselves. God has already proven that he eagerly desires to be with us and has removed the barriers so that we can enter his presence with assurance of no condemnation (Heb 10:19–22). These concepts can be difficult to believe and process, because we know that even as followers of Christ, we are still imperfect. However, I encourage you to keep studying to renew your mind with these life-changing truths.

Also, I want to try to describe how this esteem repair looks from a practical standpoint. Because the gospel is more about relationship than law, everything changes. The Bible consistently refers to us as God's children, so let's explore that concept as we consider our discussion about esteem.

Good-hearted parents will always be sensitive to the developmental process of their children. Would it make sense to scold a nine-month-old for not being potty trained yet? Would you be disappointed in your four-year-old if she had not fully grasped algebra? Would you send a guilt-producing message to your middle schooler if he had not mastered the trombone in his first year of band? Obviously not, because we understand that learning things like these are part of a process. God certainly knows this to be true and is often described in Scripture with qualities such as being patient, long-suffering, and slow to anger. Spiritual and emotional development can be even more difficult than the physical and cognitive things we must learn because they are harder to measure.

The Bible also warns us not to get into the comparison game. Galatians 6:4 says, "Each one should test their own actions. Then they can take pride in themselves alone, without comparing themselves to someone else." Common sense tells us our esteem will be good if we are living consistently with our core values. The gospel helps us balance expectations and grace in a way that we can challenge ourselves to do great things with God's help, but also to respect the fact that we are limited and flawed. Remembering that we are developing children will help us see ourselves the way God sees us.

Good parents are also able to discern when their children are not putting forth the needed effort to develop and grow their skills. Being God's child does not make us immune from a healthy kind of guilt. Guilt and shame that are designed to devalue or discourage us come from the enemy, but a true violation of a healthy conscience should result in godly sorrow. If I received a C+ in English but I did my homework and made a solid effort, a mature parent would pick up on that and accept that grade along with continuing to look for ways to improve it. If I got a C+ but I did not lift a finger and had every capacity to get an A, a healthy parent is going to feel and express some disappointment and perhaps create a consequence. But, even then, you do not get disowned for a C+, right?

My point in all of this is that as you foster your life of solitude, it requires that you like who you are becoming. If you do not, you will likely find a way to resist that life-giving time of being alone with your God, your thoughts, your dreams, and your sense of inner peace. To accomplish this task of liking who you are becoming, attention must be given to these questions:

- Do I understand that God is a patient parent?

- Do I grasp that I am like a developing child with much to learn?

- Am I undertaking the essential spiritual practices that I know will help me grow?

- Can I see visible evidence that I am a more mature person than I was last year?

If you were to evaluate your placement right now in your spiritual, emotional, and relational life, do you see yourself in preschool, elementary school, middle school, high school, college, or graduate school? There are many reasons that a person can experience delays in development. We are where we are. The goal is not to dwell on all the reasons we may feel behind, but to be committed in the present to advance and do our best to keep step with the Spirit's guidance on our journey. He is willing to pry us up out of whatever rut has captured us and help us be on our way. The psalmist said it best in Ps 40:2: "He lifted me out of the pit of despair, out of the mud and the mire. He set my feet on solid ground and steadied me as I walked along" (NLT). As you move forward, remember, there is no condemnation for those who are in Christ.

The second key element of enriching our solitude is learning to pay attention to what is called "self-talk." We all talk to ourselves, sometimes out loud, sometimes just internally. Solitude allows us to turn down all the other static in our life and to hear our own internal conversations. There is generally much to learn in becoming a good listener to ourselves.

Listening well on the inside also helps us get practice at whether the voice we are hearing in our heads is coming from our own identity, from the Spirit, from the demonic, or from someone else who has gained access to our mind. Much has been written about the mind being a battlefield. We know that in both the physical world and the spiritual realm there are numerous voices and numerous agendas out there vying for control and influence. Being a good listener to our own heart and mind helps us more effectively filter out harmful propaganda.

We get an idea of the internal goal here when we begin to look at the heart of communication in general from God's perspective.

- God's communication to us is full of grace and truth.

- His instruction to us is to "speak the truth in love"
  (Eph 4:15).

- We are to communicate for the purpose of "building
  one another up" (Eph 4:29).

When we speak to ourselves, are we speaking truth and are we building up or tearing down? It is easy to fall into the trap of rationalizations and spinning reality in our favor. Human beings are also prone to have their consciences misprogrammed because of the volume of destructive misinformation that encompasses our world. I have often been amazed at how deep our convictions can run regarding some concept that seems to have the authority of the universe behind it, but in reality, it is not even accurate. This would include self-talk such as the following:

- Someone has rejected me, so there must be something
  wrong with me.

- Certain races of people are more valuable than others.

- If I cannot do this perfectly, I may as well not even try.

- My mistakes are so bad the world will be better off
  without me in it.

It is easy to fall into the trap that my perspective is right on target when the truth has been invaded by something inaccurate. God, through the word, is consistently working to aim us toward truth, and if we keep step with his Spirit (Gal 5:25), we will find that our minds are being renewed in the direction of healthy truth.

Self-talk also needs to have a strong element of grace. In general, our internal communication will either lean toward criticism or nurture. It is not unusual for me to hear people say things out loud to themselves like the following:

- You stupid . . .
- What an idiot, will I ever learn?
- Why can't I just keep my mouth shut?

Granted, all of us have those moments where we step in it, and we are surprised by a mistake we made. But sitting with people through the years has helped me understand that lots of people have a harsh taskmaster that is relentless in its internal critique of the slightest error. Learning to forgive ourselves is far from simple. This is one reason the truth/grace model is so very important. Self-flagellation rarely inspires and energizes us to continue the journey. It is more likely to veer us off course toward discouragement and stuckness.

The internal voice of a truthful but nurturing parent allows us to be patient with ourselves while courageously facing the challenges ahead. The child within still exists in all of us, so we benefit from a growing ability to parent ourselves in ways that are gracious. For those of you who never had that voice of tender care in your life, I encourage you to be on the lookout for adding those people to your circle (more on this later), and certainly as you read Scripture, pay careful attention to how often the theme of nurture shows up in the heart of Christ—the one who has promised to never leave you or forsake you (Heb 13:5-6).

So, work toward a habit of some healthy alone time. Pay attention to the way you esteem yourself and the way you speak to yourself, and listen for God's direction as you pray, plan, reflect, and strategize for your day, week, month, and year.

Our Inner Circle

In the most well-known psalm (Ps 23), God is described as our shepherd who leads us to green pastures and quiet waters. This word picture is a perfect description of the sanctuary we need to thrive and flourish. As we have mentioned, our healthy solitude is part of our rest, and the second key part involves "our people." Jesus had his numerous followers, the twelve disciples, and even what seems to be a smaller circle with Peter, James, and John. Who is in your circle?

It is interesting to observe the way different people construct their circle. For some, it is primarily family members. Others have found their safe place in a small group experience at their church. Some just seem to need their marriage and one or two close friends. There are many options, including a certain AA meeting, a group of coworkers, a Sunday school class, a neighborhood group, an online chat room, a book club, etc.

Sanctuary involves feeling emotionally safe, developing trust, being like-minded for the most part, and genuinely liking the people with whom you are doing life. The problems that develop in our inner circle typically boil down to two main issues. Maybe I do not have enough people or enough connection to my people to enjoy true fellowship, or people are in my inner circle who disturb my sense of sanctuary and I do not know what to do with them.

There is much we could discuss about how one builds an inner circle. There is an art to building true fellowship and connection. Some people are naturally gifted at friendship and have large numbers of people who would love to be in their circle. Others are more relationally awkward and can end up feeling lonely in a world of nearly eight billion people.

The two vital skills of connection involve learning how to receive love and pour love. Remember the two greatest commandments according to Jesus involve loving. All the rest of Scripture hangs on loving God and loving others (Matt 22:37–40). Also, one of the most helpful descriptions of the Trinity that I have heard involves the Father, Son, and Spirit pouring and receiving love from one another in perfect community. If God is working to enfold us into that community—a great definition of God's kingdom—then it makes sense that learning these two vital skills would have a top priority in our lives.

It sounds simple to receive love, but have you ever tried to pour into someone who seems to have their hand over the jar? Efforts to pour end up creating a mess rather than fueling the person for the next round of challenges. To receive love, you must know you need it. You must be open to it. You must trust it. You do well to be responsive to it so that the giver knows it has been received and appreciated. In a world that beats us up in several destructive ways, the heart can close off to love, and the results are devastating.

Giving love is not without its complications either. To love well, empathy and attunement are required. One must develop a servant's heart to sacrificially pour out in a loving way. The growing cancer of self-centeredness erodes our ability to think of how our actions might affect someone else. Thus, even if we do make the effort to pour into someone, it can result in an awkward spill rather than being perceived as love. Take a few moments to reflect on your ability to receive love and to pour love. In what ways have your abilities to love well been impacted and affected by your life experiences?

I mentioned that there are two difficulties regarding the creation of your inner circle. One is finding enough people to effectively connect with so that you have an adequate support system. The other issue is dealing with someone in your circle who is ransacking your sense of peace and sanctuary. What do we do about that?

There have been many sayings that I picked up in my inner-city ministry opportunities that have been profound. One is "if you can't change the people around you, change the people around you." If our network of friends is creating turmoil, high drama, and keeping us from reaching some of our goals, perhaps it is time to think about the hard work of stepping away from this group. This is certainly at the heart of things when someone is striving to break an addiction. Old circles will likely be a source of temptation, and groups like Alcoholics or Narcotics Anonymous are there to provide new community.

The harder work of setting boundaries comes when the person in our inner circle disturbing our peace is a parent, a child, a spouse, or someone in our small group at church. It is nearly impossible to in good conscience just cut off people who are attached in deep ways, and yet, they are not someone you would choose to be in your trusted inner circle. How have you managed that?

At the beginning of this chapter, we made the distinction between our inner circle (which is a part of our sanctuary) and our mission (which is entering the messiness). For challenging people who are inextricably woven into our inner circle, we are forced to do the hard work of making the shift in our mind that this person is part of the mission rather than being a part of our peace.

Our Mission

Another of my cherished urban sayings is "you have to feed that person with a long-handled spoon." The idea is that it is not safe to get close to some people you love. This might be parallel to what Solomon had in mind in Prov 4:23 when he said, "Above all else, guard your heart." Paul also wrote in Phil 4:7 that amid the anxieties of life, the peace of God would guard our hearts and minds. Even Jesus was cautious with his trust level of unhealthy people when it was said of him, "But Jesus would not entrust himself to them, for he knew all people" (John 2:24).

The Bible makes it clear that it is possible to even love our enemies, and it is a good spiritual discipline to practice that, thus praying for them, not retaliating when we could, and being hopeful for their redemption. However, it is not wise to make yourself emotionally vulnerable to untrustworthy people. A spot in your inner circle must be earned. In our minds, challenging people need to remain in the realm of mission, not in our trusted circle.

My profession provides some valuable illustrations of the difference between inner circle and mission. I love my clients and do my best to care for them and help them reach their goals. However, for good reason, I am very cautious about how much access they have to my life outside the office. On occasion, I will hear an exuberant counselor or pastor say something like "here's my number, call me anytime day or night, don't hesitate, I will be there for you." It is a gracious offer and may make sense for a particular situation, but more often a person realizes over time that they have compromised their sanctuary and will need to go through some hard work to get proper boundaries back in place. Most of us cannot provide emergency care to everyone who needs it. I am grateful emergency ministries exist, so that I can have a strategy that shields me from burnout.

As mentioned earlier, the bigger challenge in the world of boundaries involves people who have become dysfunctional yet they are already in our circle. What do we do with them? To keep these people in the realm of mission, and at the same time guarding your heart, requires

- keeping your compassion intact,

- not taking behaviors and attitudes toward you personally,

- looking for ways to limit exposure to people to whom you are emotionally allergic,

- slowly educating people regarding what would make things better,

- separating yourself if things move into the realm of the intolerable.

I will not launch into great depth regarding this list but let's do our best to get the gist of what might be helpful. When I talk about keeping compassion intact, I think about the example of Jesus on the cross. His ability to ask the Father to forgive his persecutors (Luke 23:34) emanated from his awareness of our ignorance. Humanity is universally affected by what I like to call "relational disabilities." For numerous reasons, people can be like a bull in a china shop. There are things we are blind to, things we have not learned yet, and ways of doing things that we inherited that are not effective.

I do not want to underestimate that there are people who can be downright evil, but more often, highly annoying people are doing what they know to do and are ignorant of the damage they are creating in their wake. On the cross, Jesus makes the ultimate compassion statement and models something very important for us to learn in the process.

We also deepen our relational dilemmas when we take everything personally. Most people live their lives within patterns that would play out regardless of who they are relating to. It is possible that we may push someone's buttons in a unique way, but chances are the ugly behaviors and attitudes we are seeing would pop up just about anywhere. We are likely to be less reactive if we do not take things personally. For example, if you have a moody teenager who blurts out, "I hate you," when you say no to a request, you have a couple of options. You can take this hate message literally and personally and be deeply hurt and reactive, or you may decide to consider the source and say something like "hmm, most days you don't seem to feel that way—oh, well, I still love you anyway, but the answer is still no."

In less-than-ideal circles, there are reasons why people try to limit exposure to one another. I have seen kids who stay in their rooms, spouses who take out of town jobs, families that move across the country, people who change jobs, and numerous other strategies that limit exposure to a more tolerable level. Obviously, there are other reasons that people make these kinds of choices, but sometimes we do consciously or unconsciously create boundaries by geographical measures.

Even when we are physically present with difficult people, we can develop the ability to create invisible force fields that provide a level of protection against toxicity. Remember, your goal when with unhealthy people is to be on mission, not to make yourself highly vulnerable. Some things in life are a "labor of love," not an enjoyable experience where you let your guard down. In the field of counseling, there is an important concept called "compassionate detachment." As a caregiver, you are genuinely present and empathic, but you also develop the capacity to unplug from that person at the end of the day. If you cannot master that skill, it is likely you will struggle in completing your mission. We were not designed to carry the weight of the world on our shoulders. Only God can accomplish that.

Our mission in life will always require some degree of getting down in the weeds with people and struggling together. I love the wisdom Jesus shared with his disciples when he sent them out to serve. "I am sending you out like sheep among wolves. Therefore be as shrewd as snakes and as innocent as doves" (Matt 10:16). Our mission mindset involves never losing our compassion and our desire to see people become who God created them to be, but also requires a certain discernment and savvy to be watchful for our own safety and well-being. Much more will be said about the importance of our mission in chapter 8, where we will revisit this topic as part of our discussion about "sustaining our journey."

Case Study—Lynette

Lynette is one of the most remarkable people I have ever met. My work began with her as a client, a part of my mission. But she is the kind of person who would be a blessing to anyone's inner circle. Her presenting issue in therapy was a troubling relationship with her mother. Her mom, Ann, is a widow in her eighties. As I heard some of the stories of their interactions, I was amazed at the level of destructive power Ann seemed to wield in Lynette's world, and I am not easily amazed about such things.

It also became evident that Ann had managed to alienate almost everyone around her through the years, including her son, who lived a thousand miles away and had not spoken to her in decades. This left Lynette and her husband as the only people to help Ann as she aged and began to have more health issues.

Lynette has been very successful at everything she has done career-wise. I am not sure what her IQ is, but I know that her ability to size things up and quickly know what's going on is something I have rarely seen. She also has an enthusiastic sense of humor. While telling stories of the interactions she has had with her mom, she does a great imitation of her, and if it wasn't so sad, it would be quite entertaining.

However, with the chronic drama Ann created, Lynette had begun to experience some medical issues of her own—high stress levels, high blood pressure, and weight gain. Lynette acknowledged that she had always been very good at serving others, but not great at taking care of herself.

To give you a sampling of the kind of things Lynette had to endure, her mom would do the following:

- Feign illness to get Lynette to come to her house and provide attention, at all hours or in extreme weather conditions.

- Praise Lynette one moment for providing care and turn around and accuse her of stealing from her.

- Give Lynette a dress for Christmas that was more Ann's style (an old lady dress) and cut the tags out of it so it cannot be returned.

- Scream at the top of her lungs if Lynette said no to her demands or tried to set boundaries.

The preliminary stages of counseling for Lynette were more like a psychoeducational course on personality disorders. If you have not studied personality disorders, it can be a fascinating and helpful way to understand some of the highly difficult people who may come into your circle. There are ten classified personality disorders, all of which are high-powered defense mechanisms that greatly affect the way one sees the world.

I simply mentioned during one session that it seemed like Ann had several narcissistic traits. Lynette had some awareness of what narcissism was, but later told me she thought I was mistaken in my hunch about her mom. Then, as is her custom, Lynette dug into the literature and quickly gained a grasp of what self-centeredness looks like in its primary forms. She read one thing after another that helped her begin to find answers to what she had considered mysteries to her mom's behaviors.

Lynette also began to piece together that her mom had groomed her in many ways from early childhood to be her caretaker. One of the terms I use to describe this kind of parental narcissism is "perpetual pregnancy." This kind of parent is simply not willing to birth you and allow you to individuate toward being who God created you to be. The child is not given an identity in her own right but is seen only as an extension of the parent. Seen like any other part of their own body, the narcissistic person is happy with us only if we cooperate with what they are trying to do. If you get in their way or disturb their world too much, you will likely pay a price.

Lynette is a high achiever and she loves to make people happy. She spent a good chunk of her life enslaved to her mom's demands and felt like it was her duty, a biblical way of honoring her mom. Lynette is so talented she had, in many ways, been able to both build her life and care for her demanding mom, but it was catching up with her health-wise. Now with some mild dementia symptoms beginning to show up in Ann, some decisions needed to be made. Would she live with Lynette or would an assisted-living community be required? I rarely get so direct in my counseling style, but with all I had, I urged Lynette not to bring her mom into her inner circle. Ann is the kind of person who needs to be part of one's mission, not in close quarters where havoc could be wreaked.

Fortunately, Lynette was able to find a very competent assisted-living facility. She gets calls all the time from the staff there about what to do about her mom's latest mean-spirited behavior, but at least Lynette has maintained her home as her sanctuary and can have a life of her own for the most part.

Some family members age well and can certainly fit into the household in very manageable ways. It is a very important decision to weigh from numerous angles. One thing I have learned from working with many families through the years is that when caring for each other, we must individually define what faithful care looks like. If you allow a demanding family member to define "faithful"

79

for you, it is easy to end up feeling like the hostage of an unreason-able person's agenda. I have seen that dynamic bring some of the best caregivers to a sad place of resentment and ill-health.

If you spoke with Lynette these days, she would tell you that she is still having to awkwardly learn the skills of self-care, but she is joyful about having a vibrant life of her own where there is time for God, her husband, her children, and other friends that have earned their way into her inner circle.

PART III

Sustaining the Journey

7

The Importance of Attitude

W e have taken a close look at the direction of our trek and the kinds of obstacles that can stop us in our tracks. This last section of our study will focus on the strength to sustain our journey. There are numerous concepts in Scripture that alert us to the importance of endurance. Paul encouraged us not to grow weary in doing good (Gal 6:9). The Hebrew writer asks us to run the race with perseverance (Heb 12:1). John records the words of Jesus in the letters to the seven churches in Revelation and uses the language of "overcoming."

Being in this world but not of this world (John 17:14–16) means that we will be swimming against the current. So, figuring out how we can pace ourselves and stay the course are vital components to finishing strong. The three elements that we will cover in chapters 7, 8, and 9 involve attitude, purpose, and proper rest. From my experience, these are the three key ingredients of steady strength.

Most people would agree that attitude is an important part of the way we approach life. I have always been amazed at how some people can go through the most horrendous things in life and somehow be incredibly sturdy in the way they weather the storms. Others seem to be defeated by the normal valleys of life and always on the verge of giving up.

I would like to discuss three Biblical themes that anchor our attitudes and fortify us for whatever life throws at us. These strength-giving features are joy, gratitude, and contentment. Let us examine them one at a time.

Joy

The verses that sparked this section of our study are from a rather obscure passage in Neh 8:9-10. The story of Nehemiah is a remarkable display of endurance. He led the way in rebuilding the Jerusalem walls out of the depressing rubble. If you have not read this story in a while (or ever), I encourage you to review it. It is filled with interesting history and is one of those success stories that inspires.

What intrigues me about Neh 8 is a scene where Ezra, a teacher of the law, was reading aloud to the people. The crowd felt convicted by what they heard and began to weep. In what seems like a surprising turn of events, Nehemiah, Ezra, and the Levites tell the people not to weep or mourn on this occasion because it is a holy day—a day to be joyful and celebrative. Then Nehemiah makes this impacting statement: "For the joy of the Lord is your strength."

Notice that Nehemiah is not talking about our joy, but the Lord's joy. Stop for a moment and think about this. When you think of God, is one of your first thoughts about a being filled with joy? In God's omniscience, what is known that would lead the Creator to be joyful? Take a few minutes to record your thoughts on why you think God experiences the quality of joy.

The New Testament informs us that joy is a fruit of the Spirit (Gal 5:22), so the Spirit is also defined by this quality. Jesus is said to have endured the cross because of the "joy set before him" (Heb 12:2), another intriguing connection between joy and strength. What joy do you think Jesus was focused upon to have the strength to bear the sins of the world? It seems evident that there is something very important for us to understand about this link between joy and sustaining our spiritual trek.

Would you agree that in this world there is always something to be sad about? Not a day goes by where massive suffering is absent. People die in numerous ways. Someone is mistreated in disturbing fashion. Relational heartbreaks take place around the globe. Weather disasters create havoc. There is no escape from suffering in this broken world. So how is one to feel joy when we know this is happening?

The flip side of the coin provides a very different view. There are also amazingly good things happening all around the world. In the creation itself, we witness starry nights, beautiful sunsets, colorful birds, northern lights, stunning oceans, and mountain views. I think about a long-awaited child being born, a hardworking student graduating from school, a delightful couple finding each other and getting married or a dedicated missionary seeing people place their trust in Jesus as Savior and Lord.

Solomon was right when he said there is "a time to mourn and a time to dance" (Eccl 3:4). In this odd mixture of a glorious but broken world, we have God's permission to experience both grief and joy. It seems evident that those with a more optimistic personality would find it easier to tap into joy, but it is essential for all of us to understand that joy resides in the heart of God, and it is the Lord's desire for us to experience gladness both here and in the eternal kingdom.

Years ago, a television program named *Wide World of Sports* had a great opening line. It referred to the sports world as being a place where one could know "the thrill of victory and the agony of defeat." What an apt description of life on this planet. Since the world is filled with both, it becomes particularly important to begin to understand what brings you joy.

As someone who tends to look at life way too seriously, I have learned to pay attention to the things that bring joy and balance to life. It is important to realize that God gives us permission, even encouragement, to experience joyful things. A few items on the long list I have discovered include

- a trip with my wife to the Smoky Mountains,

- hitting a great golf shot,

- spotting a species of bird that I have never seen before,

- knowing that I have truly helped someone,

- having a sense that I am in the middle of God's will.

When you think about what fills your joy tank and strengthens you for the hard part of the journey, what is on your list?

We do well to be careful in our assessment of joy because some things can bring an initial sensation of happiness, followed by an entirely separate set of feelings. Everything in the addictive world fits this description. People get high, spend money, or have a sexual encounter because it can really feel good, but the bigger question involves whether it creates joy in the long run. I am convinced that all the guardrails the Bible gives us about behavior and choices are there to protect us from the joy counterfeits and help us maximize the real thing. What roads have you gone down in your search for joy that has led to agony?

Gratitude

First Thessalonians 5:18 says, "Give thanks in all circumstances for this is God's will for you in Christ Jesus." In case you think Paul's inclusion of the word "all" is a bit extreme, James amplifies this concept in his letter (Jas 1:3–4) by saying, "Consider it pure joy, my brothers and sisters whenever you face trials of many kinds, because you know that the testing of your faith produces perseverance." No one is perfect at applying these truths. Most of us tend to grumble when things go awry. But it is important that we understand this spiritual strategy both Paul and James are advising. The lesson we are learning here involves the intricate ties between struggle, joy, gratitude, and endurance. We have spoken a great deal about spiritual disciplines/practices already, but here we get an illustrative opportunity to see how this works. Human life is lived on many spectrums:

- Some people live to be one hundred, while some never make it out of the womb.

- Some people have an IQ of 70, while others are in the genius category of 160.

- Some people have healthy bodies while some have chronic illnesses.

- Some people have attractive personalities while others will not be popular.

- Some people are rich while some live in poverty.

- Some have numerous opportunities while others are born with two strikes against them.

The cumulative power of sin has created vast inequities in this world. The entire world system has been impacted by brokenness that we cannot fix. As much as we would like to reach the goals of justice, equality, and peace, we will only experience partial victories in this quest. Jesus himself makes incredible statements such as "the poor you will always have with you" (Mark 14:7). Some people will always be considered "the least of these" by world standards (Matt 25:37–40). Jesus warned his disciples that in this world they would have trouble (John 16:33), but he also reminded them that he had overcome the world. God has a unique way of measuring things. We are told that in the fullness of his kingdom, "the last will be first, and the first will be last" (Matt 20:16). Things will be set right.

God understands that everyone will face different challenges with various levels of strength and training to deal with what comes at us. If circumstances have the last word in forming our attitude, we are already in trouble. The conditions of this world are relative. There will always be someone who has it much easier, and someone who has it much harder. The key is learning the skill of being thankful in all circumstances. This helps us become experts at finding the good and limiting the powerlessness that accompanies victimization.

Please understand, I am not an advocate of playing internal mind games, trying to psych ourselves up into some sort of positive thinking. We feel what we feel, and typically we do not choose our feelings; they just happen. However, we do have some power when it comes to our focus. Paul mentions that we are to "take captive every thought to make it obedient to Christ" (2 Cor 10:5). The entire field of cognitive therapy is about learning to change unhelpful or inaccurate thinking patterns. Since our ultimate enemy is characterized as the "father of lies" (John 8:44), it makes sense that we discipline our thoughts toward what is true and good.

One of the most impacting cognitive disciplines is giving thanks in all circumstances. Ann Voskamp's book *One Thousand Gifts* is an excellent example of chronicling things to be thankful about even during dark or mundane days. Pain is real. Grief is real. Injustice is real, and God cares about all these things. The good news is there is gratitude to be found even in these grim times, and for those who are learning to follow Christ, the negative never has the last word. Eternal joy and glory have the last word!

One of my favorite word pictures is an agricultural one. I envision this life as our forty acres. When life is at its best, we feel like we have our full plot of land to plant, grow, and create our heart's desire. It is our territory that God has given us to cultivate and it is a source of great gratitude. However, from time to time, part of my land must be roped off. We lose access to it because of life circumstances. The following are examples of diminished joy or freedom that I have seen people go through:

- A woman has a large sum of money stolen.
- A man is told he will lose his eyesight.
- A family loses a teen to suicide.
- A person's reputation is severely damaged by a false accusation.
- A family's young adult daughter is going through harsh chemotherapy treatments.

- A young couple is told they will not be able to conceive a child.

These are all examples of loss and limitation. Instead of forty acres, you find yourself feeling like you only have five or ten. Life has shrunk and it may never be the same. Everyone's grief has its own DNA. No two grief stories follow the same exact process. But here is an important observation. The way that we look at our acreage is important to our future. People who get stuck in their grief tend to have their eyes focused on the land that is now quarantined and un-workable. People who grieve well and recover have found the ability to attend to the land that is still accessible. How many of your forty acres do you currently have access to? What is the circumstance that has stolen the biggest piece of your life? When you stand back and look at your life, where is your primary focus?

Overcomers develop a radical acceptance of the things they cannot change, and an ability to stay focused on the life that can still be lived. No loved one that we have ever lost (if given the op-portunity) would ever coach us to get stuck in our weeping and stop living. Instead, they would encourage us to get our focus on the ten or twenty acres we have left and begin rebuilding. That is not an easy process, as we discussed in our example of Nehemiah. But, to focus on what we still have is to reconnect with gratitude and productiv-ity. It is the only way to finish strong in a broken world.

I would like to think that when I am old and feeble, perhaps even in an assisted living facility, that I will be able to focus on the half acre I have left. I want to be that person who is kind to those who would help me, who prays for people and situations, and who still worships with all my heart until the day God calls me home. There is always a reason to be grateful when you soak in the fact that eternity is good beyond description, that God's grace is sufficient in this world, and the Spirit is filled with joy to share and grow within us.

It reminds me of the fascinating story in the Gospels where Peter decides he will step out of the boat to meet Jesus who was "walking on the water" (Matt 14:25–31). After experiencing this miracle of water striding for a few steps, Peter lost his focus and was distracted by the stormy waves. He began to sink. In our journey, there will always be Jesus and the storms. Where we choose to focus can have a significant difference upon whether we end up as grateful and sturdy or anxious and faltering.

Contentment

The third leg of this powerful attitude triad is a quality called contentment. Our key verses for this section are in Phil 4:11–12 which say, "I am not saying this because I am in need, for I have learned to be content whatever the circumstances. I know what it is to be in need, and I know what it is to have plenty. I have learned the secret of being content in any and every situation, whether well fed or hungry, whether living in plenty or in want."

Just as it takes spiritual practice to become grateful or focus on joy, contentment is also a secret to be learned. There is so much packed into the apostle's statement here and we do well to take some time trying to understand the depth of what he is saying. Before we begin, how would you define the concept of contentment?

Sometimes in the English language, contentment can mean a lack of drive or passion. It can be used to describe someone who has settled for less than they should. If you were using this meaning in a sentence, it might read, "Jerry was content to sit on the sidelines as life passed him by." The word Paul uses that is translated contentment would never have that connotation.

The Greek word translated "contentment" is *autarkeia*, which carries the idea of self-sufficiency, self-satisfaction, or independence. It was a concept elevated by the Stoic philosophers and was seen as being beyond need or dependency. Clearly, Paul retools this word to teach sufficiency in Christ, not simply of ourselves— thus his addition of Phil 4:13, where he states, "I can do all this through him who gives me strength."

This entire theme of sufficiency is a fascinating study that has many applications. This section of Scripture is pushing us to take a close look at our dependencies and our neediness. Paul is trying to help us understand the kinds of qualities we must have in place in our lives to be at peace on the inside.

Marriage is one of the best ways to illustrate this concept of sufficiency/contentment. Marriage is designed to be a partnership. God clearly wanted it to be the kind of relationship where we help one another. Much has been written about the needs of men and women and how we can best meet those needs. However, what happens when the need or dependency is too great? What happens in marriage when one spouse needs to save a lot of money to ward off anxiety, but the other spouse needs to spend as a method of coping with life's demands?

What if a wife requires an elevated level of order and structure in the household to be at her best, while the husband is messy, spontaneous, and quite the risk taker as part of his coping style? How might things unfold if one person is very sexual and is dependent on frequent intimate encounters, while the other has suffered extensive childhood sexual abuse and needs to avoid being triggered regarding those memories?

I like to call these "marital intersections," where one person's dependency is on a collision course with the other spouse's needs. Obviously, these kinds of crashes happen in all aspects of life including the workplace, the political realm, and the church. Two people (or two systems) that must lean too hard on certain circumstances to be okay is at the heart of the concept of codependency.

Any well-trained counselor will tell you that one of the goals we work toward in our profession is to have no needs of our own as we enter the therapeutic relationship. If I have a need to be seen as smart, to have the client like me, or to make a successful outcome happen, my agenda can get in the way of what is best for the client. If our dependencies grow too strong, they will always force us to manipulate others in order that our needs be met. I suspect we all have a story or two about being caught in that web.

I remember years ago hearing an anecdote about a phenomenon called a "two tick, no dog marriage." Imagine the disappointment of heading into a relationship, thinking this person is going to meet all your needs, only to find that they are as needy as you. If our needs and dependencies reach the level of parasitic, everyone loses, and those relationships rarely survive.

Philippians 4 teaches us that our relationship with Jesus is designed not just to meet needs, but to reduce needs so that we are characterized by giving rather than taking. Paul wanted the Christians in Philippi to understand that he was very appreciative of their assistance while he was in prison, but that even if he had not received their gifts, he would have been at peace in knowing that God would care for him whether he lived or died.

It is quite evident that he is walking the talk. Acts 16:16–40 records a phenomenal story of Paul's contentment when he was in Philippi some years before he wrote Philippians. He and his coworker, Silas, had been falsely accused and arrested. The treatment they received contained words like "stripped," "beaten with rods," "severely flogged," "thrown into prison," and "their feet were fastened in stocks."

Suppose we had had that kind of day. What might you expect the mood to be? Is contentment a word you would likely apply to yourself? I know I am not at that level of maturity yet—but at midnight, Paul and Silas were "praying and singing hymns to God." The circumstances genuinely did not seem to matter at that moment. How does one learn that secret?

Think about what Paul did not need in this situation. He did not require legal fairness to be content. He did not require sleeping in a warm bed to feel okay. He did not have to be pain-free to experience joy. Based on what you know of this story, what do you think allowed Paul and Silas to experience sufficiency and contentment?

As I sift through the principles of Scripture, here are the factors I see that increase our ability to have peace regardless of circumstances:

- Knowing that your life is moving closer to the center of God's will

- Deepening your trust that God cares and can see you through life's trials

- Entering God's mission and becoming less fearful of suffering

- Purposely being less attached to what this world has to offer

It is crystal clear from the passages that we have examined that attitude is particularly important and that we do have some level of control over our focus. Before we look at our case study, give yourself a letter grade on how you feel you are doing in the three crucial areas we have covered—joy, gratitude, and contentment.

Case Study—Lexi

When I first met Lexi, she and her two young children were homeless. She began attending classes at the crisis pregnancy center where I taught and provided counseling. I remember her asking permission on occasion to go into one of our unused classrooms and sleep on the floor because it took a while for us to find adequate housing options where she would feel safe enough to truly rest.

It did not go unnoticed that despite these dismal circumstances, Lexi would typically be smiling, and she brought life and vibrance to any class she attended. As I got to know more of her story, I discovered that Lexi's life had been quite a mix of amazing and tragic. From a family perspective, Lexi had grown up experiencing poverty, sexual abuse, and instability. However, she was very familiar with the church and faith. Lexi can pray like no other person I have ever heard.

From all I could see, she was a very good mom, but she had older children who were removed from her care by child protective services some years before. Lexi would acknowledge that she made mistakes but felt the penalty of losing her children was unjust. This loss is one of the heaviest griefs she carries.

Lexi is incredibly bright. She has had significant achievements. She worked as an EMT for a time and loves helping people. However, she has been diagnosed with a mental disorder in the past. This condition requires medication and can manifest in both thought disorder and mood disturbance. She needs support and structure in her life to be able to minimize the impact of the illness and maximize her strengths.

Lexi was married when I met her but lived separately from her husband. He had some limitations of his own, and although he was not abusive or mean-spirited, Lexi found that being with him was more like raising another child than having a husband. He was also without a home and living in a shelter.

Her faith journey has not been simple. She has had several people in her life that have been less than genuine, wearing a mask of religiosity but living out some dark realities. A church that she was part of for some time was chronically judgmental toward her when one of her children was born out of wedlock, but she found a way to graciously bow out of that group and find a church that had a better balance of truth and grace. Because Lexi reads the Bible and studies on her own, she has been able to see beyond some of the negative experiences. The love that she has for God has given her an anchor point that seems to trump any storm that comes her way.

Lexi had numerous things in her life that could have taken her down a very dark road, but her attitude was the epitome of what I have tried to describe in this chapter. Some of her personal kingdom acreage was inaccessible, but she somehow knew how to focus on her faith, the two children she had with her, the opportunities that were now opening for her, and she began to rebuild out of the rubble in an awe-inspiring way.

It took her three years to get an apartment of her own. She lived in a shelter for all that time. I remember her stories of using the community clothes washer that smelled of feces. I remember her experiences of having disruptive, unpredictable people around her. She endured occasions where people would steal the little bit she had. But through all that, she became a vital part of our downtown ministry. She was so loved by the other young women in our program that she became a part of our peer leadership team.

Lexi began to get occasional opportunities to speak, and she is a joy to listen to—so inspiring, so faithful, so humble and grateful. I would not be at all surprised if she ends up in a speaker's bureau in the future because she is that gifted and effective. Lexi has continued to face obstacles along the way, but I still hear from her occasionally and I know she has completed a medical coding course, worked to create her own sewing business, and has been reunited with at least two of her older children who wanted to connect with her after they turned eighteen.

It is so easy for us to have high expectations of how life should be and then be disappointed by reality. I have heard it said that in a world like this, where the perfect Son of God can get nailed to a tree, anything can happen. Disappointment and heartache abound, but we cannot afford to forget that joy, gratitude, and contentment are always within reach. These are the things that help us live life on life's terms and stay focused more on solutions than problems. Lexi will always be my reminder of what is possible when we live by faith and do not give in to the land of poor attitudes.

8

The Purpose of the Journey

Decades ago, Viktor Frankl, a psychiatrist and holocaust survivor, authored a fascinating book entitled *Man's Search for Meaning*. His observations from his concentration camp experience led him to believe that those who had a compelling reason to keep living were most likely to endure the unfathomable hardship that he and some of the other prisoners survived. For some, the reason may have been the hope of seeing a beloved family member just one more time. For others, perhaps the thought was an aspect of their work that still felt undone. I suspect some survivors were simply determined to not allow evil to have the last word.

It makes sense, doesn't it? If life does not feel all that meaningful or purposeful, it is likely to feel less valuable and as a result, one may not fight for it as tenaciously as a person who has a clear reason for carrying on. Take a moment before we dig deeper to answer these two questions: Do you feel your life has a clear mission? Do you believe your life is valuable?

In this section of the book that focuses on sustaining the journey, it is vital to look at the key element of purpose. It is interesting that the world of business has picked up on this concept and popularized the "mission statement." It is rare to find a business or organization these days that does not have a clear phrase or sentence to describe why it exists. The church I serve reminds me every week that we exist to "help everyone find and follow Jesus."[1]

Teamwork and energy are generated by a common purpose. If each person is on board with the vision of a group, unity and stamina are easier to maintain. Someone on an assembly line is likely to perform differently if that person is "just putting in my time" versus "building a quality truck for someone in my community." Purpose matters.

While it has become commonplace in business to talk about mission and vision, I do not hear as many people discussing this on a personal level even though Jesus certainly modeled mission statements, such as the following:

- "I have come down from heaven not to do my will but to do the will of him who sent me" (John 6:38).
- "The Son of Man came to seek and save the lost" (Luke 19:10).
- "I have come that they may have life, and have it to the full" (John 10:10).

I can still remember as a young man in my mid-twenties being on a walk and feeling like the Lord gave me a statement that has impacted my life all these years. It had four short pieces to it:

- Be as good a servant to God as I can be
- Be as good a husband as I can be
- Be as good a parent as I can be
- Get enough rest to do these things for a long time

At the time, it did not seem like something I would think of on my own. I have always been convinced it was a vision the Spirit provided for me. As with every inspirational target, I have been far from perfect in implementing this vision, but the very presence and reminder of these important life goals has kept me on task and has helped me maintain purpose and direction.

1. Okolona Christian Church, Louisville, KY.

In talking with so many believers through the years, I know it is not unusual to struggle to lay hold of a clear sense of purpose and calling. However, we do well to keep asking, seeking, and knocking (Matt 7:7) for any clarity we can receive on this important idea of a personal mission statement. Take a moment to record your mission statement based on the way you are currently living your life.

Vital Attachment

As we have already touched upon in chapter 1, love and relationships are at the core of New Testament teaching. The greatest commandments involve loving God and loving others. We know these things must be a vital part of our mission. The importance of connection is another one of those beautiful places where faith and science come together. One of the most fascinating concepts in psychology these days is called "attachment theory."

A British psychiatrist by the name of John Bowlby was the early pioneer of this work in the 1950s. He researched child development and saw the crucial importance of a secure attachment between a youngster and his/her parent/caregiver. Current research validates the fact that disturbance to the attachment of a child (things like abuse or neglect) can deeply impact one's relational well-being.

When you think about your early years of life, do you feel secure in your attachments to the key people in your life? What are you doing currently to ensure that you have a healthy support system where you get steady practice at loving and being loved?

It was in the orphanages around the world decades ago that we learned with greater clarity that you cannot just keep a baby in a crib all the time with a bottle propped up on a pillow to feed the child. Without human contact such as holding, talking, and eye contact, children do not typically flourish.

In today's culture we are learning even greater lessons about the price of disturbed attachment patterns. Caring people are deeply troubled by the things we regularly see on the news—mass shootings, record gun violence in our cities, rising suicide rates, and drug overdose deaths. Common sense tells us that these kinds of things would be extremely rare if people were healthily attached to others and felt like a part of a life-giving community.

It can be an eerie thing to talk to someone who does not love or feel loved. To be unattached can easily lead to not caring, and not caring about your life or the life of others can take one down a very dark path.

There is much debate regarding the solutions to these complex social problems, but attachment theory and the great commandments of Scripture would tell us that real progress will only be made if we work to create environments where children and youth have a better chance to feel secure and deeply loved. Things like poverty, chemical dependency, and dysfunctional parenting are barriers to secure attachment and they are not easily changed in a society. However, these problem areas must receive more focus if we are to reduce the tragic trends that now plague us. At the end of the day, learning to love and be loved must impact the formation of our personal mission.

As a point of clarity, it is obvious that some children go through the most horrific childhood trauma and, in their resilience, still somehow manage to learn key relationship skills. Some kids who have great childhoods still choose a destructive path. However, statistics tell us that healthy attachment increases the odds for a good future where harming self and harming others is much less likely. For those of you who have suffered in your early years and have had to find your way to mental and emotional health the hard way, you have my deepest respect.

Hope and Our Eternal Framework

Attachment theory reminds us of the essential realm of connection, but it can also leave us very discouraged because the social sciences have limits on what they can do to improve our world. In fact, the Bible would clarify for us that no human efforts will be adequate to heal this world of its woes. It is only in the eternal perspective that we see lasting answers to our quest for secure attachment.

In the world of faith, we learn that God is always with us. He will never forsake us. There is nothing that can separate us from God's love. We do not always feel the power of these promises, but the Bible teaches this as reality, and for those who are learning to walk with God, there is great comfort in these truths. God also has taught us to search for other people who can model this love and care. The church, when properly designed, is there to assure that those who are committed within a healthy church family receive a steady diet of love and connection. As imperfect as the church is, there are still places to be found where one can experience the necessary ingredients for healthy attachment.

Hope is at the very core of our ability to endure. I love the way Paul puts this. He says, "We remember before our God and Father your work produced by faith, your labor prompted by love, and your endurance inspired by hope in our Lord Jesus Christ" (1 Thess 1:3). There is some degree of hope available in this world, but the bountiful hope that has no limits is found only in the eternal perspective highlighted by the gospel.

This distinction between now and the future kingdom is echoed throughout Jesus's teaching. In the Sermon on the Mount, we are encouraged to place our treasures where there is true security. Everyone on the planet is susceptible to the damage of moths, rust, and thieves (Matt 6:19). Jesus makes it clear that in this world we will have trouble (John 16:33), but we are encouraged to be of good cheer because he has overcome this world system. His eternal kingdom will be free of threats, and secure attachment will be a certainty for all who are citizens there.

Colossians 3:1–2 instructs us to set our minds and hearts on things above, not on earthly things. We can lay hold of a certain amount of hope here on this planet, but it is limited and our peace regarding how things go is somewhat fragile. The mother lode of hope is bound up in the kingdom of God, not in the kingdoms of this world. It will require a new heaven and new earth to erase the corruption that has contaminated this world beyond repair.

Students of God's word have grappled for years as to why we cannot just make this world into a utopia. As we discussed in chapter 1, God is the only capable pilot who can fly this planet to it best destination. However, humanity has consistently resisted God's way and we have been determined to plot our own course. Someday, God will reclaim the pilot's seat but in the meantime, we are in for a turbulent, wobbly ride. When God came and dwelled with us through Jesus, he demonstrated his ability to heal, control nature, multiply food, put evil in its place, and even raise the dead. Every malady we face in this world today, he had an answer for—but his teachings upset us, so throughout history much of humanity said no to his leadership.

We have the Spirit to help us in our mission. God clearly holds back evil to some degree, but the Lord's biggest investment is in the coming kingdom, and it is available to all who would say, "We want your rule and your reign. By faith, we accept you as the true King of the universe." That is the source of real hope as we make our way through this challenging life in a broken world while still being on mission for God. On a scale of one to ten, how much hope do you have for your future? In what ways is this hope helping you endure the challenges you currently face?

Identifying Your Gifts

We have examined the general things that all of us need to sustain our journey. We know that we need a compelling vision that involves loving, being loved, and eternal hope for our future. We now want to turn to some of the specifics that may provide vital clues for finding our "sweet spot" of personal mission.

Once again, we gain assistance here by looking both at Scripture and psychology. The Bible states that we all have certain gifts that provide the ability to serve the kingdom in vital ways. Psychological studies have also helped us identify things like temperament, personality, and characterological traits that may define areas where we will be able to accent our strengths and minimize our weaknesses.

There are several sections of the New Testament that emphasize the idea that we have been given different gifts that help define the shape our personal mission may take. Take a moment to read these passages:

- Romans 12:4–8
- First Corinthians 12:27–31
- Ephesians 4:11–13

When you read these lists offered to us in Scripture, which gifts best describe what you have come to know about yourself? Are you a leader? Are you a helper? Are you a giver? As you consider the continuum of grace and truth, do you find yourself more on the pastoral side of mercy or the prophetic side of upholding what is righteous?

There are numerous spiritual inventories and gift assessments available online, where you can take a simple test and gain some clues about how God has prepared you to serve most effectively. I hope you can develop a healthy curiosity about your unique design and begin to explore in more depth how this knowledge impacts your sense of personal mission.

When I study the Bible, I am intrigued by the vast array of people that God called to different roles that were needed to accomplish his purposes. Doing character studies is a refreshing way to approach Scripture. Here are some good questions to ponder as you consider the hundreds of people mentioned in the Bible, such as Abraham, Ruth, Mary, and Barnabas:

- What were this person's strengths? Weaknesses?
- Are there specific ways that I am like or unlike this person?
- What might I have done if I were in their shoes?
- How did this person's faith or lack of faith show up in their encounters with God?

In addition to the search for our spiritual gifts, it is also wise to know ourselves from the standpoint of personality traits. For centuries, people have talked about the four basic temperaments: sanguine, choleric, melancholy, and phlegmatic. If you are not familiar with these terms, it will be valuable to do some research to discover their meaning. As is true in the realm of spiritual gift assessments, there are also many self-tests that can be administered to see how you score in the realm of temperament.

As a simple way of remembering the gist of the four main personalities, I have listed the following descriptions of a primary strength and weakness of each:

- Sanguine (life of the party, easily bored)
- Choleric (leader, stubborn or bossy)
- Melancholy (reflective, obsessive)
- Phlegmatic (peace-loving, procrastinator)

The value of knowing your temperament is recognizing where you are likely to fit. For example, I have known for years that I have a melancholy/phlegmatic personality. It helps me understand my journey from being a pastor to a pastoral counselor. I always enjoyed my teaching role as a pastor and my care for the people of the churches I served. But I struggled with the heaviness of a leadership role. I was too slow at making decisions because I would tend to get stuck in the analysis phase. I am very effective at seeing both sides of an issue, but the tough decisions would tend to tear me apart on the inside.

I had to learn the hard way that I have the visionary skills of a leader, but often do not have the emotional stamina to endure what good leaders must endure. I found that I am a good consultant for leaders and play a vital role in supporting leadership, but I am not wired to be the captain of a ship. These kinds of insights are not always easy on our ego, but my joy increased and my ministry endurance was extended when I accepted my limitations and utilized my strengths.

If we learn to understand the way God made us, we are more likely to craft a personal mission statement that enhances our endurance rather than one that leaves us feeling chronically discouraged and defeated, thus vulnerable to falling behind in the faith journey. So, as we summarize this chapter, helpful assignments for all of us would be

- taking a fresh look at my life purpose,

- working toward secure attachments with God and my support system,

- crafting a personal mission statement,

- developing an eternal mindset that provides a constant flow of hope,

- conducting an accurate assessment of my temperament and spiritual gifts.

If we can make progress in these essential areas, we create a scenario where giving up or burning out becomes much less likely. We are more likely to experience the memorable words of Isa 40:31 where we are told, "But those who hope in the LORD will renew their strength. They will soar on wings like eagles; they will run and not grow weary; they will walk and not be faint."

Case Study—Kate

Even before reaching the age of ten, Kate's mission was beginning to form. There was a young girl who lived next door to Kate who was never likely to be popular. But Kate had a sensitive heart for those for those who might not fit so well into this world. The two of them were best childhood friends.

At age eleven, Kate came home from school one day talking about a mission trip opportunity she heard about. She told her parents that she felt God wanted her to go. After much thought, prayer, and exploration of this mission with her family, Kate went, and had quite the adventure.

Her faith and her care for people were evident all through adolescence and her college years. As a young adult she married and was enjoying her work in the field of education. Then it started—a long season of suffering. Kate and her husband very much wanted to have children, but their first pregnancy ended in a very painful miscarriage. Kate's story of faithful endurance began.

It was not long after that season of grief that Kate began to experience numerous physical symptoms that baffled the doctors. For months, she was weak and felt horrible, but despite numerous tests, there were no clear answers. One doctor even seemed to think her illness was all in her head. However, finally the answer came that no one ever wants to hear. Kate had an exceedingly rare form of cancer.

It was no easy task to find an oncologist with experience treating this form of the disease. But Kate found a doctor she deeply respected who was willing to dig in and do the research, keeping her informed all along the way. The required procedure involved a total hysterectomy and six rounds of very strong chemotherapy. Kate was still in her twenties when all this unfolded.

Kate's family was there for her at every step, but it was a nightmarish time for all. Kate was so weak by the fifth treatment that her doctor felt she could not survive a sixth. Kate shared that during the aftermath of each treatment she felt like she would rather die than go through that again.

We have talked a great deal in this chapter about the relationship between endurance and purpose. I think Kate would tell you it was only because of her faith in God and her mission to serve that allowed her to keep pushing through. It would be nice if this story ended with a solid cure and recovery, but as life can be sometimes, Kate's future would become quite a mixture of joy and sorrow.

Kate has survived the cancer and is now fourteen years cancer free. She is truly a testimony of praising God in the storm, but it has been a difficult journey to sustain. The residual effects on the chemo have created neuropathy, issues with scar tissue, and several abdominal side effects that land Kate in the hospital at least once a year with unbearable pain. She must be super careful about what she eats and how much. Over the last year or two, she has required IV fluids daily to keep from getting dehydrated.

Despite all of this, during the last fourteen years, she and her husband adopted a son who was eight years old when he came to be with them. For three years, Kate and her husband managed a retreat center for missionaries and pastors. She became well-known in the field of pastoral care for those working in cross-cultural ministry. She even got to take a short-term trip to Africa during a season where her strength was good and her symptoms manageable.

I have been grateful to be a part of Kate's support team through the years, and she illustrates the truths of this chapter in an inspiring way. Despite all the suffering, she has a deeper purpose to live for, and it has kept her moving forward where many would have given up. Her relationship with God is vibrant and her love for the underdog is more alive than ever.

The suffering has not stopped for Kate. In fact, at the time of this writing, she is facing a fresh set of heartbreaking obstacles, but God seems to shine through her weakness. I think she would say she welcomes the time when the Lord will call her home, but until he does, she will keep doing what she can to love God and love people. And oh, by the way, the young childhood friend that I mentioned earlier—Kate reconnected with her recently and she is now a missionary working with Native American children. The purpose and depth of meaning to life never runs dry for those who take their calling seriously.

9

The Concept of Rest

I n examining the essentials of sustaining our spiritual trek, we have looked at the importance of attitude and purpose. Now we come to the final element of endurance, which is proper rest. I dare say that in our world of striving, efficiency, and productivity, one might not have expected that a key ingredient of a successful journey involves rest and proper pacing.

God obviously knows this about human beings, and from the very beginning of the Bible, the idea of rest is a central element. The creation account is fascinating in that after the six days of speaking things into existence, Gen 2:1–3 says that God rested and thus set apart the seventh day as unique.

There is nothing in Scripture to indicate that God experiences weariness or has the need to sleep—quite the contrary. So, it must be assumed that this concept of Sabbath is an example for us. The Old Testament law places lofty emphasis on the day of rest and its emphasis is nailed down by being a part of the Ten Commandments (Exod 20:8–11).

We have studied God's characteristics in this book because seeing God accurately is so important to a healthy faith. God's attention to rest for the creation is one more amazingly attractive feature. From my experience, numerous Christians have ideas that put God in the category of a taskmaster. The Lord wants us to pray without ceasing, to evangelize the world, to deny ourselves, to think of others first, to suffer for his name's sake, and to be perfect as the heavenly Father is perfect (Matt 5:48).

While these concepts are descriptive of the Christian walk, it is fair to say that no taskmaster has ever said to his subjects, "Hey, I want you to be sure that you place intentional focus on resting and renewal so that you can be at your best as you accomplish your mission." Is there any part of you that is surprised that God is so interested in rest? How do you feel you are doing overall at your personal balance of mission and rest?

Jesus and the Sabbath

As you read the Gospel accounts, one of the things you will notice is much tension developed between Jesus and the Jewish religious leaders regarding the Sabbath. This happened because the interpretation of the Old Testament Sabbath laws had become legalistic. What God intended as a principle that would bring rest and true worship had instead become one more laborious set of rules by which to judge one another.

There is something within us as human beings that wants to create concrete guidelines that can be measured and enforced. The Pharisees of Jesus's day were not the only people to fall into this trap. Every generation faces the temptation to hammer on the letter of the law, while God teaches us to learn to discern "the spirit of the law" (2 Cor 3:6), which is the law's proper application.

For example, there was more than one occasion where Jesus healed someone on the Sabbath day. The teachers of the law viewed this as evidence that Jesus could not possibly be the Messiah because this healing would be considered work on the Sabbath, thus a sin. Jesus tried to teach them that he was Lord of the Sabbath (Matt 12:8) and knew how to apply the spirit and intent of the law, but most were too entrenched in their burdensome view of the Sabbath to truly hear Jesus's appeal.

It is an interesting shift that takes place as one contrasts the Sabbath in the Old Testament and the New Testament. The day of worship for the Jewish people was the Sabbath day, Saturday, and the roots of this go all the way back to the emphasis of rest in the creation account. However, for first-century Christians, the day of worship became the first day of the week, Sunday, which seems to be tied to the resurrection of Jesus.

This surprising shift in the day of worship is a powerful connection point in our faith history. The Old Testament builds its day of worship upon God as Creator, and the New Testament builds its day of worship on God as re-Creator or Redeemer. This concept is played out in Rev 4–5. These are the great worship scenes in heaven, where John gets to peek through the open door into the throne room of God.

In Rev 4, there is a scene of great praise and God is praised as the Creator (4:11). In Rev 5, there is a very similar worship experience where the focus is upon "the Lamb." Adoration and glory are given to Jesus and a new song is sung, because he has "purchased for God persons from every . . . nation" with his blood (5:9).

I have always been fascinated with the way the Bible ties the past, present, and future together. The Old Testament had its purpose and introduced us to the concept of Sabbath. The New Testament era that we now live in focuses on Jesus and redemption and helps us understand that the Sabbath is a broad, sweeping principle that is not to be applied legalistically. Interestingly, there is a final worship scene in Rev 19 where God is worshipped as King. This is where the Lord's reign is fully implemented and his will prevails. It is the beginning of the new heaven and new earth where all is made new. This is what the Hebrew writer refers to as the ultimate Sabbath rest (Heb 4:8–10). As you consider these passages and the various ways the Bible emphasizes rest, worship, and Sabbath, what jumps out at you as the most important applications for your life?

Ministry and Self-Care

For those of us who are in the people-helping professions (teaching, counseling, missions, social work, etc.), it is not unusual to hear talk about self-care. Why is this? Being in the trenches with people is demanding. From my experience it creates a different kind of tiredness. I feel for my friends who have physically demanding jobs. If you are out in the elements of summer heat or winter cold, or lifting heavy things all day, your body is going to need to recuperate. But leading and working with people can be emotionally exhausting.

I cannot tell you how many times I have heard the illustration that takes place while you are getting your flight instructions. If the cabin loses pressure, grab the mask where oxygen is flowing and put on your own mask first before trying to assist someone else with their mask. It makes sense, right? You are not going to be good to anyone else if you are unconscious. This concept is applied to people-helpers on a regular basis. Take care of yourself first, lest you lose your ability to be helpful to others.

In careers and volunteer roles where the burnout levels can be high, we do well to learn how to rest emotionally, spiritually, mentally, and physically. All of this can be a bit tricky. The Christian faith instructs us to be on mission and to put a high value on sacrificing for the sake of others. How do we balance loving others as ourselves (Matt 22:39)? How do we practice self-care without being selfish?

Before we continue, take a few minutes to assess your current level of feeling rested.

Take note of the statement that describes you most accurately:

- I feel good levels of energy as I head into most days.
- I feel tired quite a bit, but I can still make it through the day.
- It is all I can do to make myself keep going day after day.
- I dread getting out of bed most days.

Our minds, bodies and emotions have amazing ways of letting us know that we need to pay attention to something. God designed them to be signaling devices that help us in our assessment of the life we are living. People who are self-aware of things like stress levels and weariness have a leg up on those who are grinding through life. It is easy to fall into the trap of "working with your head down," paying no attention to how what we are doing is impacting our health and wellness. Good self-care starts with becoming a student of our energy level, our thought process, and our moods.

As energy costs have risen through the years, it has become wise for businesses and homeowners to conduct energy audits. These audits might study things like the efficiency levels of heating and cooling systems, the types of lighting, various kinds of doors and windows, and insulation. Using this model can help us learn to monitor our personal energy usage.

As individuals, we all have different levels of energy to start each day. Some people are wired like the Energizer Bunny and never seem to run out of pep in their step. Others may be dealing with a chronic illness or the aging process and have a smaller fuel tank to draw from. It is important to understand this because we are prone to compare ourselves to those who are the best in any area. We then become discouraged if we do not measure up. Energy levels are unique to each person, and although there may be things that we can do to increase our energy level, those changes usually happen slowly.

Once we have an idea of the size of our personal energy reservoir, we can begin evaluating where our energies are being spent. As you pay attention to your daily routine, you can often begin to have an idea of what drains you and what qualifies as restful or even energizing.

As a way to practice these evaluation skills, consider the list below and assign numbers between one and ten. The low end of the scale represents things that leave you feeling drained, while the high end of the scale indicates activities that help you feel rested or renewed.

- Attending a social event such as a wedding and reception
- Praying
- Exercising
- Talking on the phone with a friend
- Doing a chore around the house
- Playing with children
- Mowing grass
- Playing a board game
- Going to church
- Scrolling through your phone
- Having an in-depth conversation with someone you love
- Writing in your journal
- Listening to music
- Balancing your checkbook
- Driving across town
- Visiting someone in the hospital
- Public speaking

As you can hopefully tell, there is no "one-size-fits-all" approach to rest. What is restful for one person may suck the life out of another. However, for all of us the goal is to have ample energy day by day to live life and fulfill our purpose. Burnout, discouragement, and what I call a "full-life bankruptcy" are altogether preventable. We have the clearest of instructions from God that chronically running out of steam is not the plan for us. We will have days and even seasons where we may face weariness, but it does not have to be our way of life, and we cannot give exhaustion the last word.

Two Biblical Examples of Exhaustion

I have always been appreciative that the stories of Scripture portray the life of God's people with such honesty and authenticity. Even the heroes of the faith had deeply fallible moments. This helps us understand more about the grace and patience of God as human beings make their way through this challenging world. Two such heroes are Moses and Elijah. One thing they had in common was a low moment in their leadership roles where both cried out to God with a death wish. Here it is in their own words.

Moses said, "I cannot carry all these people by myself, the burden is too heavy for me. If this is how you are going to treat me, please go ahead and kill me—if I have found favor in your eyes—and do not let me face my own ruin" (Num 11:14–15).

It is said of Elijah that "he came to a broom bush, sat down under it and prayed that he might die. 'I have had enough, Lord,' he said. 'Take my life; I am no better than my ancestors'" (1 Kgs 19:4).

Stress, exhaustion, and the weight of ministry can have this effect on all of us. It is a powerful reminder that sustaining our journey is of the utmost importance. If this kind of despair can be experienced by men of this caliber, we are all vulnerable. Can you remember a time in your own journey where you were on the edge of burnout? If so, take a moment to record those memories.

For Moses, the context is the masses of people who were unhappy, grumbling, wailing, and looking to him for answers. For Elijah, it was literally the aftermath of a great mountaintop experience followed by a death threat from an evil queen. He was running for his life. We could spend time looking at the circumstances in depth, and I would encourage you to go back and read these amazing stories. But the real lesson in perseverance and hope comes from studying God's response to these two exhausted servants. Let us examine that in detail.

In Num 11, when Moses cried out to God in his exhausted desperation, there was no lecture from God. There was no scolding or condemnation. God simply reminded Moses of a lesson he had to learn years before. It was in Exod 18 where Moses's father-in-law,

Jethro, shared an insight regarding delegation. Jethro recognized that Moses tended to take on the heavy load of the people all by himself and recommended a very practical solution.

One of the primary causes of burnout is taking on more weighty matters than we can sustain. Forgetting to train others or struggling to delegate can get us into troubled waters. Would you say you are one of those people who has a hard time entrusting others with the workload?

God was gracious to Moses in Num 11. He told him he would take "some of the power of the Spirit" that was on Moses and place it on seventy elders who could assist Moses in this time of heaviness. Sometimes things in our lives can change quickly, and we end up with a significant imbalance and a season where one is extremely busy. But this story is a reminder that God wants us to always be on the lookout for how we can recover and not allow exhaustion to be a way of life.

Elijah's recovery is equally fascinating. He wants to die, and the first thing God does is provide food and some sleep. Sometimes it is easy to neglect the simple things. I do not know about you, but I know for me, I can become a different person when I am chronically tired. Everything tends to look darker when you are too "crispy around the edges." Self-care begins with simple things like adequate sleep, good nutrition, and balanced exercise. We may be able to neglect them for a time, but it will catch up with you if you try to get away with cheating on these basics.

The next thing that stands out in the 1 Kgs 19 story is that Elijah is convinced he is alone in his zeal for the Lord's way. Everyone has their own version of Superman's kryptonite—something that robs our power and leaves us weak and vulnerable. For many people, their kryptonite is feeling alone or isolated. There is a reason God has designed community for us. There is a reason that solitary confinement is one of the most dreaded punishments in our world. Having no one around us that understands or gets us is very taxing. Support systems are of the utmost importance in our effort to finish strong.

Not surprisingly, God intervenes in this very important sphere of Elijah's life. God reminds him that there are seven thousand others who have not "bowed their knee to Baal" (1 Kgs 19:18), and the chapter concludes with Elijah meeting Elisha. This is perhaps the most endearing mentoring arrangement we read in Scripture—two kindred spirits doing the difficult prophetic work of God in a remarkably successful way. Elijah completed his mission on a high note.

As if God's gracious prescription for Moses and Elijah were not enough, something very interesting happened regarding these two servants in the New Testament. There is a riveting story in the Gospels, often referred to as the "transfiguration." Matthew, Mark, and Luke all recorded this event. At a time when Jesus was beginning to prepare his disciples for his death, Peter, James, and John got to experience Jesus in his glory. Jesus's followers were witnesses to amazing things, but they still only saw Jesus in common form—as one of us in every way.

However, on this day, it was deemed that they would get a glimpse of Jesus as he really is—God in the flesh. Guess who was there with Jesus and his three disciples? You got it: Moses and Elijah. It is likely that this duo symbolizes the law and the prophets, but I find myself wondering if during a time when the disciples would face hardship and exhausting grief, did God have an additional purpose in selecting these two heroes to be present?

As hard as leadership was for Moses and Elijah, and as much as they despaired on occasion, here they were alive and vibrant, experiencing the glory of Jesus. I find myself thinking this story is recorded for all weary servants to know that God's grace is sufficient, and we will be delivered to that eternal promised rest as we learn to trust in our darkest times. Does this make you want to finish strong?

Case Study—Rob

When I first met Rob, he was a worship leader in the student ministry at a large church. We recognized rather quickly that we had a great deal in common and that our views of ministry were very similar. We both love ministry and love people but are both introverts at heart. Rob loves music and had been mentored by some very talented people. However, he found himself restless in his current role, and was puzzled as to why he sometimes dreaded Sunday mornings and often felt fatigued, which was not typical for him in general.

As we began poking around, exploring his feelings, and evaluating this energy drain he was experiencing, we stumbled onto some valuable insights. Rob realized it was very difficult to motivate the current student group of which he was a part. He acknowledged that in general he was more comfortable working with adults. There was also an issue of worship style. The church where Rob served was very contemporary and emphasized a high energy worship experience. At the core, Rob is a very deep, reflective person and would have preferred to focus on meaningful lyrics, times of quiet, and a more meditative worship.

I watched him for months wrestle with this internal tension, in a sense trying to fit a square peg into a round hole. There would be occasions of ministry highlight, and Rob really wanted to stay in his current position. He is a very loyal person. However, his waning energies and diminishing hope that things would be different continued to take their toll on his spirit. Our word picture for his dilemma was "being trapped in a box canyon." He felt stuck with no way out of a role that was meaningful but "was not him."

As Rob tried to describe his torn-ness to the lead pastor at his church, Rob received some helpful counsel that he should prayerfully attend to the feelings that he was experiencing. It was clear the church did not want to lose Rob since he was seen as a very valuable part of the team. But if worship leading in a larger contemporary church did not fit well, what would? Rob began to expand his horizons regarding his career options. He ultimately landed on a decision to enter a graduate school that specialized in the field of spiritual formation and direction. I agreed with Rob that this would likely be an investment that would provide a fascinating chapter to his life and ministry.

The Spirit of God confirmed this decision in several ways—one being that Rob felt alive again at the deepest level. He stayed in his student worship position for a time while he continued to explore his career options. He noticed that he was better able to stay positive and serve well in that capacity. Rob's life became an illustration of the power of hope, as we studied in chapter 8. Just knowing that some new adventure of faith was coming was enough to help him endure until another door opened.

And it did open. Some months later, Rob got a call from a church he had applied to that was looking for a worship pastor. This was a smaller church of two hundred that placed high emphasis on spiritual formation and a deeper walk with Christ. The interview process with this church created an immediate bond, and this church that was a thousand miles away was incredibly eager to have him join their team. As Rob and I continued to meet, we would often talk about the grace that God had shown, and the amazing providence of this journey from burnout to full scale energetic joy.

Rob has been in that new setting for a year or two now, and it is so encouraging to watch. He loves graduate school, leading worship, writing songs, and working with youth. Yet, with all those things to do, I know of no one who is more committed to the Sabbath principle. He views the Sabbath as a spiritual practice and protects his Monday tradition to rest and worship better than anyone I know.

Rob's experience holds several lessons for all of us. Our souls do not flourish in every circumstance. We cannot always change our circumstances immediately. At times, we must simply hold on and lean on God's strength to persevere. However, it is always wise to pay attention to our life rhythms, and if we experience a waning energy, let the exploration begin. Seek guidance from those you trust and look for the energy drains together. See burnout for the threat and enemy it is and apply the principles of the Sabbath to find and protect your mission that God has given you. Do not give up easily, but do not be afraid to explore new options. Be loyal, but do not be loyal to the neglect of a new calling.

Conclusion

A s I explore a way to properly conclude this book, I find myself wondering who might read it, what your circumstances may be, what is coming at you in the way of hardship, and what you are really feeling at the deepest levels—you know, all those things that counselors tend to be curious about. I also find myself hoping that there has been something you have read that has provided those "aha experiences" that keep you asking, seeking, and knocking for the answers God has for your life. So, whether you have read this book on your own, as a part of a small group study, or in a classroom setting, I pray that it has been a blessing to you.

One of the greatest joys of this project for me has been getting to reconnect with some of the people I have had the privilege of counseling. Working together to craft their stories accurately was a great reminder of the power and blessing of true teamwork. I suspect all of you know that not every counseling story ends successfully. There are numerous factors that go into the progress or failure of therapy. Every counselor has their share of days in the office that are heavy and deeply disappointing. We also face our own insecurities and the realization that we have made mistakes.

I chose life-changing journeys for this book, not to set an unrealistic expectation, but to let everyone know that it is possible, and to illustrate the key principles of this study in a practical way. The nine cases that I have shared are there to inspire and remind us that getting from Egypt to the promised land still happens.

We began our trek with a realization that Jesus taught there is "a way that leads to life" (Matt 7:14). In fact, Jesus is "the way" (John 14:6). There is no greater mission than to point people to Jesus. Learning to love him and truly be his disciple is at the core of finding life. Our goal in this study has been to search both Scripture and life experience to flesh out some of the details of a successful journey on this life-giving road with Christ.

I realize that my effort to integrate psychological theory and principles into this book carries some degree of risk. Psychology has numerous principles that tend to fly in the face of biblical truth. I am not advocating that we immerse ourselves in psychology with all its secular roots. However, like all sciences, there are truths to be gleaned that are in sync with the Bible. God's word is always the standard by which we measure. Things we discover that reinforce and illustrate scriptural principles can be useful. If the findings from other fields of study conflict with biblical revelation, they are to be set aside. I like the statement that advocates "all truth is God's truth." So, exercise caution, but do not be afraid of science, as long as you understand that a solid biblical foundation is your standard.

I am convinced that if we march in the right direction (section 1), avoid the pitfalls (section 2), and can keep moving (section 3), we are certain to land in the vicinity of where God wants us to be. Let me close with this prayer for you:

Lord, we know that in the beginning you created a perfect world. We also know that perfection will be restored someday. Those who place their trust in you will get to see you in the fullness of your glory. You truly are the giver of every good gift that exists in this universe.

But we know that we live in this long interlude called human history, where imperfections touch every aspect of our lives. The battle between good and evil is real, and we are impacted by the suffering this battle creates. Our lives are filled with very good things and very painful things, and we need help navigating our way through this war, so that our faith remains intact, and we finish strong.

We want those who are suffering to know that you have entered the pain with us through your Son, Jesus. You have promised sufficient grace as we undertake the life of being your students. Help us learn to love you with all our hearts. Help us be teachable so that we are not closed off to your direction. Help us realize our journey is unique and may not look like everyone else's. Help us find our true identity in you.

Lord, help us not to become defensive in destructive ways that ultimately weigh us down. Guide us to use the emotions you gave us in a way that is constructive, not destructive. Help us choose our closest friends wisely, so that we do not feel alone on the journey. Sustain us with an attitude of joyful hope because we have not lost sight of our glorious future. Give us a purpose that inspires and lends meaning to life so that we endure and persevere.

And Lord, as you do so well, lead us to green pastures and quiet waters so our souls are restored. Provide those amazing seasons of refreshing so that our mission to serve you well continues until you call us home. We love you and are so grateful that you hear our heartfelt cries. In Jesus's name, Amen.

Made in the USA
Monee, IL
06 June 2024

59433023R00079